Farshore

First published in Great Britain 2024 by Farshore
An imprint of HarperCollins*Publishers*,
1 London Bridge Street, London, SE1 9GF
www.farshore.co.uk

HarperCollins*Publishers*
Macken House, 39/40 Mayor Street Upper,
Dublin 1, D01 C9W8, Ireland

BEANO.COM

A Beano Studios Product © DC Thomson & Co Ltd. (2024)

Written by Danielle Mercer
Design and additional illustration by Matt Carr

Additional imagery used under licence from Shutterstock.com

ISBN 978 0 00 861651 9
Printed in the UK by Bell & Bain Ltd.
001

All rights reserved. No part of this publication may be reproduced, stored in a retrieval system, or transmitted, in any form or by any means, electronic, mechanical, photocopying, recording or otherwise, without the prior permission of the publisher and copyright owner.

Stay safe online. Any website addresses listed in this book are correct at the time of going to print. However, Farshore is not responsible for content hosted by third parties. Please be aware that online content can be subject to change and websites can contain content that is unsuitable for children. We advise that all children are supervised when using the internet.

This book is written for entertainment purposes only and HarperCollins*Publishers* is not responsible for the consequences of any pranks that you pull. The pranks in this book should always be performed while under the supervision of an adult and you should never perform a prank on someone who would not enjoy it.

Adult supervision is advised for the recipe activities within the book.

If this symbol appears on a page, it means that you should seek the assistance of an adult to help you complete the activity.

FSC
www.fsc.org

MIX
Paper | Supporting
responsible forestry
FSC™ C007454

This book contains FSC™ certified paper and other controlled sources to ensure responsible forest management.

For more information visit: www.harpercollins.co.uk/green

CONTENTS

Welcome to Beano Boredom Busters 5

INDOOR MISCHIEF 6

Poo, Glorious Poo! 10
Who Sham-pooed on You? 11
Pen of Invisibility 12
Pass the Dog Parcel 13
A Present You Can Count On 14
Must Dash! 15
Sweet, Sweet Codes 16
Run, Water, Run! 17
Ink-redible Blooms 18
I Could Draw Him In My Sleep 19
Tick, Tick, Shriek! 20
Where's the Wally? 22
One Kid's Rubbish is Another Kid's Treasure .. 23
I Kid You Knot! 24
You've Never Cooked Better! 26
Slice to See You 28
Oh Heck, Oobleck! 29

CRAFTY CREATIVITY 30

Tell It as It Isn't 33
Taking the Biscuit 34
Paint a Pizza Picture 36
I'd Rather Pie! 38
Evil-Veg Smoothie 40
Roger's Dodgers 42
Trick-or-Treat Cupcakes 44
Armpit Fudge 46
A Hug in a Mug 48
Day of the Banana Bread! 50
Butch Butcher's Rock 'n' Sausage Roll 52
Ice Cream Supreme 54
Hap-pea Shooter 56
Draw. Laugh. Love. 58
Get Animated! 60
Stick in the Spud 62
The Plot Thickens! 64
A Wheely Good Decoder 66
Instrument Until Proven Guilty 68
New Kid on the Sock 70
A Flipping Good Time 72

OUTDOOR ADVENTURES 74

Come on, Den 76

It Wouldn't Bee Home With You 78

I'm Rooting For You 80

A Mo-mint-ous Occasion 82

Feed the Birds 84

Get a Head 86

Less Talk, More Chalk 88

Scavenger Found it Yet? 90

Scavenger Pigeons 92

Keep it Up 94

Thinking A-cloud 96

ORGANISED MAYHEM 98

Penny Hunters 100

Stuck in the Mud 101

Capture the Flag 102

Escape Room 104

Forty Forty 106

Shripwreck 108

Imposter Game 110

Don't Drop It! 114

Mummy Dance Off 115

The Saucepan Game 116

Flour Face 117

French Cricket 118

Sardines 120

The Chocolate Game 122

Frisby Golf 124

Wink Murder 125

Goodbye! 126

Ever wanted a treasure trove of pranks to shock your mates with and make your family laugh? What about whipping up some nosh with extra bite? Do you fancy playing some games that are snot to be taken lightly? Or are you just looking for something to chase the boredom away?

Well, look no further! The residents of Beanotown have just the cure for boredom, and they have all brought their ideas along to make sure you are never far from pulling an awesome prank or playing a fun game. Bring a spare pair of pants, ditch the adults and get ready for a blamazing time!

I HAVE LOADS OF GAMES FOR YOU TO PLAY AND FOR ME TO WIN!

MY IDEA OF FUN IS FAR SUPERIOR TO ANYONE ELSE'S.

JOIN ME AND MY FAMILY FOR PRANKMAGEDDON!

INDOOR MISCHIEF

POURING WITH RAIN? BIT OF A SNIFFLE? SICK HAMSTER? DON'T LET THAT STOP YOU FROM HAVING FUN! THERE'S LOTS OF CHEEKINESS AND SHENANIGANS YOU CAN GET UP TO INDOORS. ROLL UP YOUR SLEEVES AND TURN THE PAGE TO GET BUSY ...

POO, GLORIOUS POO!

Pull the ultimate poo-rank with this brown playdough recipe. Bea likes to pull her clean nappy off and hide her playdough poop somewhere in the house for her parents to find. In her poo-fessional opinion, it's the best prank known to toddlers!

IS PLAYDOUGH OR POOP?

I NOT TELLING!

STUFF YOU NEED:

• 8 tbsp plain flour, plus extra for kneading
• 2 tbsp salt
• 60 ml warm water
• 1 tbsp oil
• Food colouring

EQUIPMENT:

Large plastic bowl
Wooden spoon
Small measuring jug

INSTRUCTIONS:

1 In your plastic bowl, mix the plain flour and salt together.

2 Measure out the water in a jug, then add a few drops of food colouring and the oil. Chances are, you don't have brown food colouring (who does?!), but you can make the colour brown with equal amounts of red and green food colouring. Or just experiment with the colours you've got - you're bound to make brown eventually!

3 Add the brown liquid to the flour mixture and stir together until fully combined.

4 Sprinkle some flour on a clean surface and pop your dough on it. Knead it for a few minutes until it is perfectly squishy and gross.

5 Now for the fun part. Squeeze the dough into a poo shape and hide it somewhere in the house for someone to find. Then wait for the squeals of disgust!

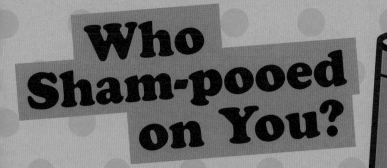

HELLO FELLOW TROUBLEMAKERS! READY FOR SOMETHING THAT IS EASY PEASY SHAMPOO-SQUEEZY? WELL, I PLAYED THIS TOTALLY BLAM PRANK ON MY SISTER HEENA LAST WEEK AND WANTED TO LET YOU IN ON MY GENIUS-NESS. (SHE DID GET ME BACK, BUT YOU'LL HEAR MORE ABOUT THAT LATER!) SHE WAS IN THE SHOWER FOR AGES, TRYING TO FIGURE OUT WHY NOTHING WAS COMING OUT OF THE FULL BOTTLE OF SHAMPOO. I WAS LAUGHING SO HARD, I NEARLY WET MYSELF.

STUFF YOU NEED:

- Shampoo bottle
- Cling film

INSTRUCTIONS:

1 Take the shampoo cap off.

2 Get some cling film – not much – just a bit bigger than the top.

3 Wrap the cling film tightly over the hole where the cap was. (Make sure it can't be seen under the cap.)

4 Replace the cap and check the shampoo doesn't come out when you tip it upside down.

5 Put the shampoo bottle back where it was.

6 Leg it! The next person to use the shampoo won't be able to get any out!

PEN OF INVISIBILITY

Right, you sneaky set of super sleuths! If you're like me, then you can sniff out a mystery at the mere mention of biscuits. One super-cool trick I use to keep any nosey no-gooders off my tail is to write secret messages. IT'S REALLY SQU-EASY!

Angel Face

TOP SECRET

STUFF YOU NEED:

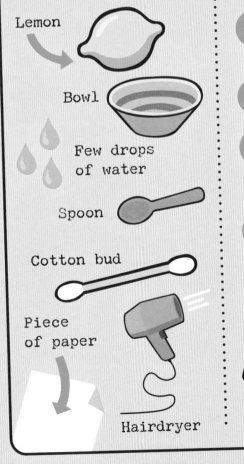

Lemon

Bowl

Few drops of water

Spoon

Cotton bud

Piece of paper

Hairdryer

INSTRUCTIONS:

1 Cut your lemon in half and squeeze the juice of one of the halves into the bowl.

2 Add a few drops of water and stir with your spoon.

3 Dip your cotton bud into the lemony water and write your secret message on the paper.

Angel Face Rules!

4 Now leave your message to dry. As it dries, your secret message will magically disappear.

5 For someone to see what you've written, they'll have to aim a hairdryer on a low heat at your paper to make your message reappear . . . Ta da! Make sure an adult helps you with the hairdryer and keep it away from water (and the back away from your hair, in case it eats it!).

PASS THE ~~DOG~~ PARCEL

> Gno, this isn't a game where you pass the dog around. Games aren't just for you lot, you gnow! One of my favourite things to play is pass the parcel with my best mate Dennis and the other Dinmakers. You can gnever go wrong if it's filled with sausages from Butch Butcher's shop, but I s'pose other doggy treats would do too.

STUFF YOU NEED:

DOGGO
BIG CHEW for the centre
(A dog would be useful!)

DOG TREATS
YUMMY GNASHOs

2 or more OLD TEA TOWELS or T-SHIRTS

MUSIC
♫ 'Who Let the Dogs Out'* ♫
*Always a good one!

INSTRUCTIONS:

1 Ask an adult very nicely whether you can have a couple of their old tea towels, or ask to use two of your old T-shirts that don't fit anymore. You should probably also warn them that they'll never be usable again . . .

2 Place the first tea towel or t-shirt flat on a surface. Take some dog treats and a big chew, and sprinkle them in a long line down the middle.

3 Take the long end of your tea towel or t-shirt and start rolling it up, so that the treats wind up all along it. Tie it loosely in a big knot.

4 Add treats to your second tea towel or t-shirt and roll it up in the same way. Then take your original knot and tie this second roll around it to form a loose ball (that your doggy pal could undo).

5 Pop some music on and get your friends or family to pass the parcel around until it gets to your four-legged friend. Now stop the music and watch as your dog tries to unwrap each delicious layer!

A Present You Can Count On

Symptoms:

Last week, I ran into my house. It really hurt. And when I was having my head bandaged up afterwards in St. Somewhere Hospital, *I saw someone come in with a missing finger. There was blood everywhere!* But it gave me a really good idea for a prank.

Stuff you need:

Scissors
Small box with lid
Cotton wool
Red paint
Paintbrush

Instructions:

1) Use your scissors to cut a hole in the bottom of your box. Not too big - just big enough for your finger to fit through. Be careful not to actually cut your finger off! On second thought, grab an adult to help you with this bit!

2) Fill the box with cotton wool, leaving the hole uncovered.

3) Paint the middle of the cotton wool with red paint, so it looks like blood (yuck!).

4) Put your finger up through the bottom of the box, so it looks like it's been cut off. Put the lid on. Now go and shock your mates with this gross prank! When they open the box, they'll think you've gifted them a severed finger!

MUST DASH!

AS I'M THE SECOND MOST IMPORTANT PERSON IN BEANOTOWN (MY FATHER IS THE MOST IMPORTANT), I GET WHATEVER I WANT. AND LAST SUMMER, I MADE BERTIE COME ON A MORSE-CODE TRAINING CAMP WITH ME, SO WE COULD START PLOTTING AGAINST DENNIS IN SECRET. I'M FEELING GENEROUS TODAY, SO THOUGHT I'D LET YOU KNOW HOW IT'S DONE. JUST DON'T TELL DENNIS AND HIS FRIENDS!

INFO:

Morse code was used by the army during the Second World War to send and receive secret messages. It was made up of lots of dots and dashes, representing each letter of the alphabet. See if you can work out Walter's message using the code below. Each word is separated by a /.

A •—	J •———	S •••
B —•••	K —•—	T —
C —•—•	L •—••	U ••—
D —••	M ——	V •••—
E •	N —•	W •——
F ••—•	O ———	X —••—
G ——•	P •——•	Y —•——
H ••••	Q ——•—	Z ——••
I ••	R •—•	

—— • •• — / —— • / ••— ••• —— / ••• •— —— •—• —•——'••• /

•••• • •—•• •• —•—• ——— •—• — • •—•/••—• ——— •—•/

•• ——— —— • / •—•• •—• ——— — — •• —• ——•/!

Sweet, Sweet Codes

Breaking codes is what I'm best at, and I need to do it a lot in my Investigating Agency. So, if you enjoyed doing snotty Walter's challenge, you're going to LOVE mine! And as cakes are my favourite, I've made you a cupcake-themed puzzle, just to give you something to sniff out.

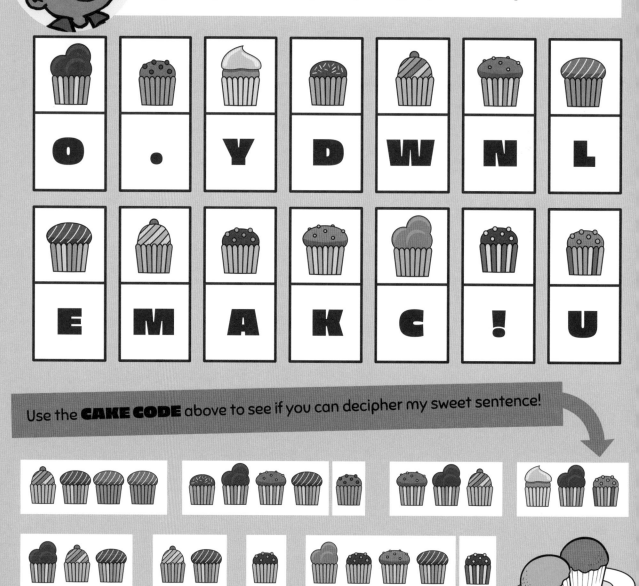

Use the **CAKE CODE** above to see if you can decipher my sweet sentence!

Answer: Well done. Now you owe me a cake!

RUN, WATER, RUN!

Pranks with clever props are super awesome, but not everyone has a dad who owns a joke shop! So I thought I'd let you in on a water-ific joke that I played on my mum. It doesn't need much, but it had her running across the room faster than Billy Whizz. Oh, and you get extra points if other people in the house fall for it too!

STUFF YOU NEED:

6 bottles or glasses of water

x6

x3

3 pairs of trainers

INSTRUCTIONS:

Make sure no one else is around, then position all your trainers on the stairs, so they look like they are walking down them. Next, put a full bottle (or half glass) of water inside each shoe (being careful not to spill any). Now loudly shout out:

'QUICK, QUICK! THERE'S WATER RUNNING DOWN THE STAIRS!'

Step aside and watch as your panicked prank-victim runs into the room, expecting to see a tsunami of water whooshing towards them!

INK-REDIBLE BLOOMS

I always have a few tricks up my sleeve — and I don't just mean my epic skateboarding backside power-slide — and here's one I'm giving you for free. I had my mum completely befuddled when her freshly bought white flowers mysteriously turned blue overnight! She was actually super mad. How was I to know she needed white flowers for an event with the mayor?

STUFF YOU NEED:

FOOD COLOURING (ANY COLOUR)

FOOD COLOURING

FRESH WHITE FLOWERS (CARNATIONS WORK BEST)

VASE

WARM WATER

INSTRUCTIONS:

1. Fill the vase halfway up with warm water.

2. Add 15–20 drops of whichever food colouring you've chosen to the vase. You could even use a few small vases and try out different colours in each one.

3. Cut the flower stems at a slanted angle — ask an adult for help — and place them in the vase.

4. Leave the flowers in the water and keep checking to see when the transformation begins. It should take between six and eight hours, so leaving them overnight is a good idea.

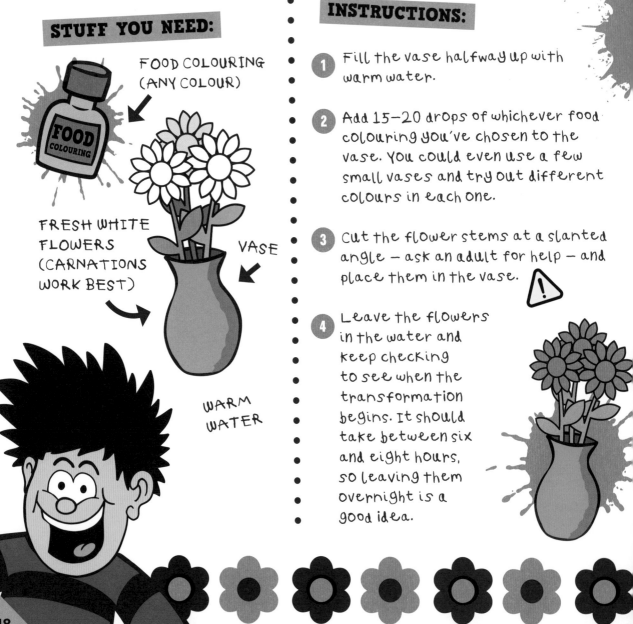

I COULD DRAW HIM IN MY SLEEP

Hey! You're in Walter's Fan Club too? Well, he does have the most epic ideas about everything (plus the best private pool). Though I did overhear Angel Face telling Jenny the other day that Dennis said that Roger was saying that Walter stinks. Well, I can tell you for a fact that he smells as divine as always. What I like to do when I'm not with Walter is to draw him. And I know him so well that I can draw him with my eyes shut! Can you?

STUFF YOU NEED:

· Pencil
· Paper

INSTRUCTIONS:

1. Place your pencil on your piece of paper and close your eyes. Now try to imagine the face that you want to draw. Start by drawing the eyes and other features of the face that show emotion. Keep your eyes closed!

2. Next, attempt to draw the shape of their head around the facial features. No peeking!

3. When you've finished, open your eyes and have a look at your creation. Does it look like them?

4. Now try again, but this time don't take your pencil off the paper. Perhaps you could even try adding some glasses and a crazy hat?

WALTER WORK OF ART!
by Bertie!

TICK, TICK, SHRIEK!

> HEY THERE. I DON'T HAVE LONG, I'M JUST IN THE MIDDLE OF WATCHING A MAKE-UP TUTORIAL ON YOU-HOO, BUT I WANTED TO TELL YOU ABOUT A COOL BATH BOMB THAT HAS A HIDDEN SURPRISE IN THE MIDDLE. THE PERSON YOU GIVE IT TO WILL THINK IT'S SUCH A LOVELY GIFT, AND THEN WHEN THEY USE IT . . . WELL, JUST FOLLOW THE SCREAMS. IT'S PERFECT FOR GETTING SOMEONE BACK FOR PRANKING YOU. YES, I MEAN YOU, HARSHA!

STUFF YOU NEED:

40 g cornflour
100 g bicarbonate of soda
50 g citric acid
2 tbsp coconut oil
¼ tsp an essential oil
(I use orange essential oil)
2 tbsp water
A few drops of liquid (not gel)
food colouring, any colour
4 small plastic creepy crawlies

EQUIPMENT:

Mixing bowl
Whisk
Plastic moulds
(yogurt or pudding pots work well,
or you can use silicone cupcake cases)

INSTRUCTIONS:

ASK AN ADULT VERY NICELY TO HELP YOU MAKE YOUR BATH BOMBS – AND ALSO TO NOT TELL YOUR VICTIM ABOUT WHAT'S INSIDE!

1 Put the cornflour, bicarbonate of soda and citric acid in a bowl. Whisk until combined.

 2 In a separate small bowl, pour in the coconut oil, your chosen essential oil, water and food colouring, and mix well until they're all combined. **BE SURE TO USE ONLY A TINY BIT OF FOOD COLOURING – YOU DON'T WANT TO STAIN THE BATHTUB!**

3 Now, take your time with this bit. Very slowly, and just a little at a time, so that it doesn't get too fizzy, add the wet mixture to the dry ingredients. Whisk each time you add some until the mixture is wet enough to clump together and keep its shape when pressed in your hand – but not too wet that it's sloppy!

4 Spoon your mixture into your chosen mould and push it in tightly. Add your chosen plastic creepy crawly to the middle and cover it over. Smooth over the top with a teaspoon.

5 Leave your bath bombs to dry for 2-4 hours. Take care when removing them from the moulds.

NOW THEY ARE READY FOR YOU TO GET YOUR OWN BACK!

AAARGH!

WHERE'S THE WALLY?

If you are as dangerously attractive as me, then everyone will probably want more pictures of you around the house. Let's be honest, it's only fair on other people that they get to enjoy you more, so let's spread the joy! My friends seemed speechless with appreciation when they found all the photos I'd hidden around their houses.

STUFF YOU NEED:

Pictures of yourself in various small sizes

Tape

Kid-friendly scissors

INSTRUCTIONS:

Cut your head out of every photo. Then find funny places to hide them, such as on the toilet roll, in the newspaper, on fruit, over other people's faces in family portraits, etc. If you hide lots, then the prank just keeps getting funnier as more and more are found!

One Kid's Rubbish is Another Kid's Treasure

My mum wants me to tidy my room, but I have a much better idea! I'm going on a treasure hunt! What are you waiting for? Find an eye patch, draw a skull and cross bones to attach to your top, and get hunting. Treasure hunts are the best, ye landlubbers! Why's that? Because they arrrrrr!

Treasure Hunt Around the House

Can you find something . . .

- [ ] green
- [ ] to sit on
- [ ] that smells bad
- [ ] with eyes
- [ ] that makes a noise
- [ ] to eat with
- [ ] to read
- [ ] you can wear
- [ ] that lights up
- [ ] with a nose
- [ ] that turns on and off
- [ ] orange
- [ ] that tells the time
- [ ] with a pattern on it

- [ ] to write with
- [ ] you can see through
- [ ] blue
- [ ] squishy
- [ ] with wheels
- [ ] with paws
- [ ] black
- [ ] with buttons
- [ ] soft
- [ ] round
- [ ] rough
- [ ] yellow
- [ ] that sinks in water
- [ ] you can eat

- [ ] that closes
- [ ] white
- [ ] that smells good
- [ ] alive
- [ ] made of metal
- [ ] that holds things
- [ ] crooked
- [ ] brown
- [ ] shiny
- [ ] red
- [ ] square
- [ ] purple
- [ ] that floats on water
- [ ] that opens

If you manage to find everything, then you are officially blamazing!

# I Kid you Knot!

DIAGONAL LASHING KNOT

Used to tie two sticks together in a cross.

1 Place two poles or sticks in a cross and tie a simple knot around them both diagonally.

2 Wrap your rope diagonally around the two sticks in the same direction a few times.

HALF HITCH KNOT

Used to tie rope around an object.

1 Loop the rope around an object.

2 Place the shorter end of the rope over the other end.

REEF KNOT

For if your rope isn't long enough and you need to add another one.

1 Cross two lengths of rope in an X shape.

2 Take the upper section of the lower (red) rope and cross it over the other (blue) rope.

3 Take the lower piece of (red) rope and loop it over the top of the other (blue) rope, so that your ropes look like a W.

24

YOU NEVER KNOW WHEN YOU MIGHT NEED A GOOD STRONG KNOT TO TIE DENNIS – I MEAN, THINGS – TOGETHER. SO HAVING THE KNOWLEDGE OF A FEW DIFFERENT ONES UNDER YOUR BELT COULD BE VERY USEFUL. I'VE PRACTISED ALL OF MINE ON – I MEAN *WITH* – BERTIE.

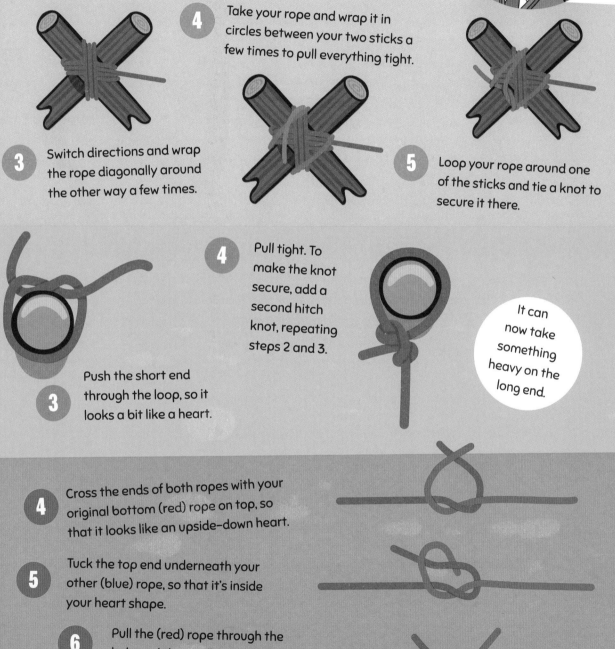

4 Take your rope and wrap it in circles between your two sticks a few times to pull everything tight.

3 Switch directions and wrap the rope diagonally around the other way a few times.

5 Loop your rope around one of the sticks and tie a knot to secure it there.

4 Pull tight. To make the knot secure, add a second hitch knot, repeating steps 2 and 3.

3 Push the short end through the loop, so it looks a bit like a heart.

It can now take something heavy on the long end.

4 Cross the ends of both ropes with your original bottom (red) rope on top, so that it looks like an upside–down heart.

5 Tuck the top end underneath your other (blue) rope, so that it's inside your heart shape.

6 Pull the (red) rope through the hole and then pull both ends tight. There you have it – a longer rope!

YOU'VE NEVER COOKED BETTER!

Got spots? Skin feeling as rough as Gnasher's fur? How awful for you. It's not actually something I would know about, but then skin as gorgeous as mine doesn't just happen on its own, you know. I spend a good few minutes every day making sure I look this fabulous, and one of my regular face-routine tricks is to make a face mask recommended to me by Bananaman. He seemed lost for words at my beauty.

PLUG!

Please check the mask mixture on a small area of skin before applying to your face, just to make sure you're not allergic to any of the ingredients.

Banana Face Mask

(general all-rounder)

STUFF YOU NEED:

1 medium-sized banana

8 tbsp plain yogurt

2 tbsp honey

INSTRUCTIONS:

Mash everything together in a bowl to make a smooth paste. Gently apply to your face and neck, and leave it to set for 10–20 minutes. Rinse off with warm water and pat dry with a towel.

Lemon Face Mask

(blackhead buster)

STUFF YOU NEED:

2 tbsp lemon juice

1 tbsp honey

1 tbsp extra virgin olive oil

INSTRUCTIONS:

Mix together all your ingredients in a bowl. Gently apply to your face and wait for 15 minutes. Rinse off with warm water and pat dry with a towel.

Top Tip: To really give your face some love, be sure to moisturise afterwards!

SLICE TO SEE YOU

Listen in, fellow citizens and brave visitors. Ever alert for a call to action, I always have a trusty banana to hand, and I happen to have a nifty banana trick that may a-peel to you. 'A magic trick involving a banana?' I hear you cry! Yes, indeed, I can in fact make a banana even more magical. Imagine, if you will, peeling back the skin on your favourite yellow fruit and finding it's already been cut into slices for you. What?! But that's impossible! Do not fear, my little friends. I, Bananaman, will teach you how it's done. This trick had Chief O'Reilly baffled for weeks!

STUFF YOU NEED:

· Banana
· Cocktail stick

1 Find a seam on the banana – these are the ridges that stick out a bit and run down the outside of the fruit's skin.

2 **WITH THE HELP OF AN ADULT,** carefully push the cocktail stick through the skin and all the way into the banana. Make sure you don't puncture through the other side.

3 Wiggle the cocktail stick carefully from side to side inside the banana, taking care not to damage the entry point. This will give you your first slice.

WIGGLE!

4 When you feel happy that the first slice is done, pull out the cocktail stick carefully. Now move down the banana seam to where you want to make your next slice and reinsert the cocktail stick.

5 Repeat steps 2 and 3 until you've made all the invisible slices inside the banana.

6 Remove the cocktail stick and give your banana to an unsuspecting person. As they peel it, watch as their eyes grow bigger than my muscles*.

*Not actually possible. My muscles are ginormous!

OH HECK, OOBLECK!

WHEN I WAS STUDYING FOR ONE OF MY (FOUR) DEGREES, OUTRAGEOUSLY DIFFICULT CHEMISTRY, I CAME ACROSS A RATHER FUN EXPERIMENT USING JUST CORNFLOUR AND WATER. IT WAS A NICE CHANGE TO PLAY WITH SOME GOOEY STUFF, RATHER THAN HAVING TO HIDE FROM SOME SLIMEY STUFF. BUT THAT'S ALL IN MY TOP-SECRET RESEARCH STATION THAT ABSOLUTELY NOBODY KNOWS ANYTHING ABOUT. AHEM.

STUFF YOU NEED:

- 75 g cornflour
- 50–60 ml water
- Tablespoon
- Tray or bowl
- Apron

CORN Flour

INSTRUCTIONS:

1 Pop your apron on and put a heaped tablespoon of cornflour on a tray or into a bowl.

2 Add the water slowly, and only a bit at a time, stirring it together until the cornflour looks like a very thick liquid.

3 Now it's ready to play with! Try stirring it or rolling it into a ball in your hand and see what happens.

IT'S GOO-REAT FUN!

CRAFTY CREATIVITY

RAINING OUTSIDE? WI-FI DOWN? CRAVING CREATIVITY? WELL, WHAT ARE YOU WAITING FOR? CHUCK ON YOUR APRON OR OLD CLOTHES AND LET'S GET CRAFTY!

Tell It as It Isn't

Are you a secret super pranker? A quick-thinking creator of all things destructive and disgusting? Excellent, then we're going to get on! Something I do to remind me of my pranking genius is to keep an awesome comic diary. And the best bit? It doesn't have to be accurate! You can make your life even more epic and hilarious in your comics than it is in real life.

Stuff you need:

• Plain diary or notebook
• Pencil or fine ink pen

Instructions:

1 Think about something that's happened to you recently, it could be good or bad, fun or embarrassing, big or minor. No one needs to see this if you don't want them to, so it can be for your eyes only.

2 Draw out some boxes in your book and have a think about what you're going to put in each one. For example, if you took a bus into town, you could start with a drawing of you standing at the bus stop, then one of you on the bus, then another at your destination (I'm sure your comics will be much more exciting than that though!).

3 Try to keep the drawings simple. See if you can capture the event in just a few sketches.

4 Write some speech and thought bubbles around your drawings. You don't need many words, as the images will explain what's happening in your story. The words should support what the images show.

Here's one I did earlier!

Practise makes perfect, so see if you can do this every day for a week. Who knows when you might enjoy looking back on the time you put a whoopee cushion on Grandpa's chair!*

*Oh wait, that was me!

Taking the Biscuit

Hello duckies! A biscuit a day keeps the doctor away, that's what I've always said (it also makes people want to visit you – Dennis is always coming round to snaffle some of my homemade biccies). Plus my melting moments are talked about all over Beanotown, they're that good. So untie your mum, put your bike back outside and get ready for some baking with Gran!

ALLERGY AWARE!
Do not try this where allergies may be an issue.

MENACE IN THE KITCHEN!

EVERY WIDL YELPS!

INGREDIENTS:

200 g unsalted butter, softened
125 g caster sugar
1 egg
½ tsp vanilla extract
250 g self-raising flour
50 g rolled oats

EQUIPMENT:

Baking trays x2
Baking paper
Mixing bowl
Wooden spoon
Small glass or bowl
Wire cooling rack

INSTRUCTIONS:

Yum!

1 Ask an adult to preheat your oven to 180°C/160°C fan. ⚠️

2 Line a couple of baking trays with baking or parchment paper.

3 Cream the butter and sugar together until light and fluffy.

4 Crack the egg into a small glass or bowl – no one wants egg shell in their biscuits! Then add the vanilla extract and mix it in with your butter and sugar.

5 Add the flour and mix until it all comes together into a ball of dough. Don't be afraid to get your hands in there to get the last bits incorporated.

6 Split your mix into 12–14 small balls. Measure your oats into a bowl and roll your biscuits in them until coated. Then place them on the lined baking tray – spaced out as they will spread in the oven.

7 Now ask an adult to bake your biscuits for 10–12 minutes or until they have begun to turn a golden brown. Then leave them to cool on a wire rack. ⚠️

PAINT A PIZZA PICTURE

A RATHER FUN AND ARTY THING TO DO – NO, NOT 'FARTY', DENNIS – IS TO CREATE A PICTURE ON TOP OF A PIZZA. YOU COULD DO SOMETHING LIKE, OOH I DON'T KNOW, COPY A FAMOUS PIECE OF ART USING SWEETCORN FOR SUNFLOWERS AND MAKE IT SO GOOD THAT YOU COULD SWAP IT OUT FOR THE REAL THING, AND NOBODY WOULD NOTICE! IMAGINE DOING THAT! AHEM. BUT ANOTHER GOOD ONE IS TO MAKE A PORTRAIT OF SOMEONE . . .

INGREDIENTS:

PIZZA BASE:

300 g natural yogurt
300 g self-raising flour
1 tbsp olive oil

TOMATO SAUCE:

250 ml tomato passata
1½ tsp tomato purée
½ tsp oregano
½ tsp salt
¼ tsp sugar
1 tsp olive oil

TOPPING:

150 g mozzarella cheese, sliced
50 g cheddar cheese, grated
30 parmesan cheese, grated
Extra toppings (optional)

EQUIPMENT:

Bowl
Wooden spoon
Rolling pin
Flat baking tray

ALLERGY AWARE!
Do not try this where allergies may be an issue.

1 Ask an adult to preheat the oven to 240°C/220°C fan. To make your pizza base, measure out the yogurt, flour and olive oil into a bowl and mix them together until they form a ball of dough.

2 Split your dough into even balls, then flour your surface, grab a rolling pin and roll them out into thin circles. Pop them onto baking trays, ready for toppings.

3 Make your tomato sauce by measuring the tomato passata, tomato purée, oregano, salt, sugar and olive oil into a bowl and mixing them together with a wooden spoon – simple!

4 Add a thin layer of tomato sauce to your pizza bases, stopping just short of the edges for the crust.

5 Figure out which picture you're going to make, then prepare whatever toppings you're going to use to create it. For instance, you could make a portrait of someone using cheese for skin, olives for eyes, a slice of mushroom for a nose and a strip of pepper for a mouth. Get creative!

6 Ask an adult to put your pizzas in the oven and bake for 10–12 minutes until your crusts are browned and your cheese is perfectly melted and bubbling. Then enjoy your masterpiece!

THE DENN-IZZA!

SPINACH or ROCKET

GREEN PEPPER

RED PEPPER

SLICED MUSHROOMS

CHEESE

BLACK OLIVES

I'D RATHER PIE!

The best things in life are ... pies! That's what I think anyway. There's nothing you can't put in a pie (apart from your grandma – that would taste horrible). When I'm not chilling out with my best mate Paul the potato, I love making people happy by baking them pies. It's a pie-tastic thing to do!

Pie Face

Paul the Potato

INGREDIENTS:

3 white onions (ask an adult to finely slice these for you)

2 ready-rolled shortcrust pastry sheets

25 g unsalted butter

BUTTER

3 eggs

400 g mature cheddar, grated

ALLERGY AWARE!
Do not try this where allergies may be an issue.

EQUIPMENT:

Saucepan
Mixing bowl
Baking tray
Glass
Pie dish
Spoon
Pastry brush
Fork

INSTRUCTIONS:

1 Ask an adult to help you melt the butter in a saucepan over a low–medium heat and then fry the onions in it for 10–15 minutes. Stir them frequently until they are soft. Pop the onions into a mixing bowl and leave them to cool.

2 Preheat the oven to 190°C/170°C fan and ask an adult to put a baking tray inside to warm up. Beat two of your eggs lightly in a glass, then stir them into the cooled onions. Add the cheese and season with a bit of salt and pepper.

3 Take one of your pastry sheets and unravel it. Use this to line a pie dish, pressing it up the sides. Trim the edges, and if there are any tears or cracks, use the offcuts to patch these up.

4 Carefully spoon the filling into the pastry case. Pat it down gently with the back of the spoon. Beat your remaining egg and brush a small amount over the pastry rim.

5 Take your second pastry sheet and place it over the top. Use your fingertips to seal the edges. Trim off any extra bits, then pinch around the edge (leaving a crimped look) or press with a fork to seal it fully. To allow steam to escape when cooking, poke a small hole in the middle. Now brush the top with the leftover beaten egg. If you want to get decorative with your pie, you could use any extra pieces to create shapes. Add these to the top of your pie and brush them with egg too.

6 Ask an adult to place the pie onto the hot baking tray in the oven and bake for 40–50 minutes until the pastry is golden brown. Carefully remove from the oven and leave to cool for a few minutes before serving. You can also leave it to cool completely and eat it cold. If kept chilled, you can enjoy it for up to four days.

EVIL-VEG SMOOTHIE

SOMETHING I WHIZZ UP FOR MY FAMILY ON A MONDAY MORNING IS MY FAMOUS VEGETABLE SMOOTHIE. YOU MIGHT TURN YOUR NOSES UP AT THE IDEA, BUT IT'S SO DELICIOUS THAT EVEN DENNIS AND BEA DRINK IT! JUST REMEMBER TO PUT THE LID ON THE BLENDER — WE'RE MAKING A SMOOTHIE, NOT A FACE MASK!

INGREDIENTS:

500 ML MILK (CAN BE NON-DAIRY)

MILK

1 BANANA

2 HANDFULS OF FRESH BABY SPINACH

1 FRESH OR FROZEN MANGO (CHOPPED)

HALF AN AVOCADO (STONE REMOVED)

ALLERGY AWARE! Do not try this where allergies may be an issue.

INSTRUCTIONS:

Put the spinach, avocado, mango, banana and milk into your blender and ask an adult to blitz it until smooth. Serve immediately.

Any leftovers can be frozen in lolly moulds for a yummy ice lolly.

WHIZZ!

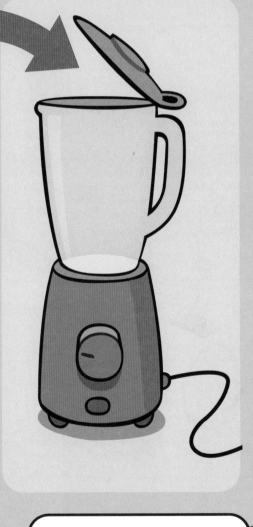

DON'T WORRY, IT TASTES BETTER THAN IT LOOKS!

ROGER'S

The only thing that will get me up in the morning is the fresh smell of prank potential . . . and jammy biscuits. Unfortunately, I love them so much, we're always running out of them and I can't be bothered to go to the shop to buy more. So I make them! You're probably thinking, 'But Roger, isn't baking more effort?', and you'd be correct, but baking is far more fun!

Ingredients:

100 g unsalted butter, softened
175 g caster sugar (plus extra for sprinkling)
1 large egg (NOT OSTRICH LARGE!)
1 tsp vanilla paste or essence
200 g plain flour (plus extra for dusting)
370 g strawberry jam

Equipment:

Wooden spoon
Mixing bowl
Rolling pin
Biscuit cutters
Baking tray
Baking paper
Wire rack
Butter knife

ALLERGY AWARE!
Do not try this where allergies may be an issue.

CASTER SUGAR

BUTTER

JAM

VANILLA ESSENCE

PLAIN FLOUR

DODGERS

Instructions:

1. For the biscuits, use a wooden spoon to mix the butter and sugar together in a bowl until light and fluffy. Add the egg and vanilla, and beat again until fully mixed. Scrape the edges of the bowl down to make sure everything is fully combined.

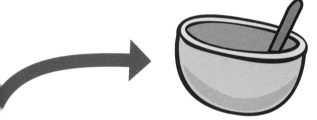

2. Add the flour and fold into the mixture, until it forms a ball of dough. Now, roll the dough out onto a floured sheet of baking paper until it is about 5 mm deep. Carefully lift the sheet onto a baking tray and place in the fridge for 10 minutes to firm up.

3. Remove from the fridge and, using a 6 cm cutter (any shape will do), cut out your biscuits. You will need an equal number of them – one for the top and bottom. Cut a 2 cm shape or hole in the centre of half of the biscuits.

4. Use your dough offcuts to make another batch of biscuits. If the mixture gets sticky, just pop it back in the fridge to firm up again.

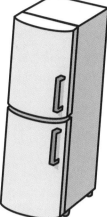

5. When all your shapes are ready, space them out across a couple of lined baking trays and place them in the fridge to cool for 10 minutes.

6. While cooling, ask an adult for help with the oven. Preheat the oven to 190°C/170°C fan, then bake your biscuits for 7 minutes. Remove from the oven and sprinkle caster sugar over the biscuits. Put all the biscuits back in the oven and cook for another 5 minutes. Now, place them on a wire rack to cool fully.

7. When they are cool, spread jam on the bottom biscuits and sandwich them together with the top biscuits. If stored in an airtight tin, your biscuits should last for 2–3 days – more than enough time to gobble them all up!

TRICK-OR-TREAT CUPCAKES

OH, HELLO THERE! SO GOOD OF YOU TO DROP BY. I DON'T OFTEN GET TO TALK TO FOLK – THEY ALWAYS LEAVE IN SUCH A HURRY . . . NORMALLY SCREAMING AND AWKWARDLY COVERING THEIR UNDERGARMENTS. I'M NOT SURE WHAT THEY EXPECTED WHEN THEY VISITED MY HAUNTED CASTLE – A FAIRY GODMOTHER? I'M HOPING MY TRICK-OR-TREAT CUPCAKES WILL BE JUST THE THING TO SEE THEM FLOCKING TO MY NEW BOGEYMAN CAFÉ INSTEAD OF RUNNING FOR THE HILLS. WILL THEY GET A CUPCAKE WITH CHOCOLATE CHIPS OR RAISINS INSIDE?

INGREDIENTS:

- 100 g unsalted butter
- 100 g caster sugar
- 2 large eggs
- ½ tsp vanilla essence
- 100 g self-raising flour, sifted
- 100 g chocolate chips
- 100 g raisins
- Icing sugar for dusting

RAISINS

CHOC CHIPS

EQUIPMENT:

- Cupcake cases
- Cupcake baking tray
- 2 mixing bowls
- Wooden spoon
- Food mixer
- Sieve
- Dessert spoons

ALLERGY AWARE!
Do not try this where allergies may be an issue.

INSTRUCTIONS:

1 Pop 8 cupcake cases in a cupcake tray and ask an adult to preheat the oven to 190°C/170°C fan.

2 Place the butter and caster sugar into a bowl or food mixer and beat until light and fluffy.

3 Add the eggs one at a time. Once fully combined, add in the vanilla essence.

4 Fold in the sifted flour, making sure it all gets mixed in around the edges.

5 Now, put half of your mixture into a second bowl.

6 Add chocolate chips to one bowl and raisins to the other. Fold them in well.

7 Using two dessert spoons, spoon your mixture into the cupcake cases, so they are half full.

8 Ask an adult to pop them in the oven to cook for 15-20 minutes. You'll know when they are done if you put a cocktail stick in the middle and it comes out clean. If it comes out with mixture on it, then they need a bit more time in the oven.

9 Once cooked, place the cupcakes on a cooling rack and dust with icing sugar. Now no one will know which ones have raisins in and which ones have chocolate in. Of course, if you like raisins, you'll be fine either way!

TOP TIP:

If you really want to have a laugh with these, leave out the chocolate chips and raisins, and instead scoop a hole out of every baked cupcake and add jam to all but one, which you can fill with ketchup! Pop the bits of cake back in and no one will be able to tell which is which. You won't want to miss someone eating that trick cake!

45

Armpit Fudge

What More is There to Spray?

What's brown, squidgy, makes a squelchy sound and yet is somehow delicious? Yes, that's right, it's ... armpit fudge! My best friend Danny once pretended he and my dog Sniffy were eating poo – I nearly barfed. But now I've made this loads of times! It's a right laugh to do and tastes great. So get squelching!

Stuff you need:

Large plastic zipper bag
2 tsp cocoa powder
50 g icing sugar
¼ tsp vanilla extract
1 tbsp unsalted butter
2 tsp cream cheese

COCOA POWDER

VANILLA EXTRACT

ICING SUGAR

CREAM CHEESE

BUTTER

ALLERGY AWARE! Do not try this where allergies may be an issue.

TO AVOID ACTUAL ARMPIT FUDGE, MAKE SURE YOUR BAG DOESN'T SPLIT!

Instructions:

1 Measure all your ingredients into a sealable plastic bag.

2 Squeeze all the air out of the bag and zip it up tightly.

3 Pop the bag under your arm, right up into your armpit, and get mushing!

4 Keep squelching until all the mixture is combined into a chocolatey fudge.

5 Grab a spoon and DIG IN!

SQUISH!
MUSH!

IT LOOKS LIKE SOMETHING I MIGHT MAKE!

A HUG IN A MUG

Hello cookies! How berry nice to see you. We pride ourselves on being able to make our students' tummies growl with joy as they leave the dinner hall. Not many people can claim that chicken nugget. It's true, the little darlings all run from their seats, screaming with excitement to tell their friends how wonderful our food is. This mug cake is a quick sugar fix for anyone who has stuck around long enough for dessert!

Stuff you need:

Mug

Fork

Microwave

3 tbsp self-raising flour

2 tbsp caster sugar

1 tbsp cocoa powder

1 tbsp oil*

4 tbsp milk

1 tbsp chocolate spread

ALLERGY AWARE! Do not try this where allergies may be an issue.

*Can you guess what oil the Olives like to use? Olive oil, of course! Perhaps that's why their mug cakes taste so weird ... We suggest using vegetable or sunflower oil instead.

OLIVE SPRAT

OLIVE PRATT

Instructions:

1 In a mug, measure out the self-raising flour, caster sugar and cocoa powder. Mix well with a fork.

2 Now add the oil and milk, and mix it all together until smooth. Then add a generous dollop of your favourite chocolate spread on top - this will sink down and give you a melting middle! The Olives like to put mustard and sweet-chilli jam in their mug cakes, but perhaps that's why no one hangs around for pudding!

3 Place your mug in a microwave. Ask an adult to cook on full-power for 1-2 minutes, or until there's no cake batter at the bottom. Poke a spoon in there and it drag away from the side to check it's cooked at the bottom.

4 Leave to stand for a minute, then tuck in!

PING!

YUM!

1:30

49

DAY OF THE BANANA BREAD!

DO YOU EVER FEEL LIKE THERE'S ANOTHER 'YOU' THAT YOU KEEP HIDDEN FROM OTHER PEOPLE? AND DO YOU FIND THAT WHEN YOU EAT SOMETHING IN PARTICULAR, THAT IT BRINGS THAT 'HIDDEN SIDE' WHIZZING OUT IN A MEGA-TIGHT BODY SUIT AND A CAPE? NO WAY! ME TOO! HAVE A GO AT ONE OF MY FAVOURITE RECIPES AND SEE WHAT MY SUPERFOOD DOES FOR YOU.

INGREDIENTS:

- 140 g unsalted butter, softened
- 140 g caster sugar
- 2 large eggs
- 140 g self-raising flour
- 2 very ripe bananas, mashed
- 1 tsp baking powder
- 100 g chocolate chips (optional)
- 50 g icing sugar or 50 g chocolate
- 2–3 tbp water

ALLERGY AWARE! Do not try this where allergies may be an issue.

EQUIPMENT:

- Loaf tin
- Baking paper
- Mixing bowl
- Wooden spoon
- Masher (or fork)
- Wire rack

1 First, ask an adult to preheat your oven to 180°C/160°C fan.

2 Line a loaf tin with baking paper (the base and sides).

3 Mix the butter and caster sugar together until light and fluffy. Add the eggs slowly, along with a bit of the flour.

4 Add the mashed banana, remaining flour and baking powder, and fold it all in. If bananas aren't already the best flavour ever, chuck in some chocolate chips and stir them in.

MAKE SURE YOU'VE MASHED YOUR 'NANAS!

5 Carefully pour your mixture into the loaf tin and ask an adult to bake it in the oven for roughly 50 minutes.

6 Around 30–40 minutes into the baking, check your bread every 5 minutes or so by inserting a skewer. If the skewer comes out clean, then your bread is cooked.

7 Ask an adult to remove your bread from the oven and allow it to cool in the tin for 10 minutes.

8 Once cool, take the banana bread out of the tin and place it on a wire rack – this can be fiddly, so I usually ask an adult to help me with this bit as well.

9 Now for the icing. Put your icing sugar in a bowl and add 2–3 tsp of water. This should make it runny. Or, if you've already proven yourself a chocolate–lover, melt some chocolate in the microwave in 30–second bursts instead.

10 Carefully pour your chosen icing over the top of your loaf and allow it to set.

11 Have some stretchy clothing and a cape to hand in case your inner superhero suddenly bursts out. It's always good to be prepared!

Butch Butcher's Rock 'n' Sausage Roll

If you just can't help falling in love with sausage rolls (and Elvis!) then this is the recipe for you. And for those of you out there with suspicious minds, then I suggest a little less conversation, a little more action please. So surrender to your taste buds and try these amazing sausage rock 'n' rolls. They're certainly always on my mind! Enough Elvis? Oh alright.

SAUSAGE ROLLS GO LOVELY WITH A BIT OF KETCHUP!

INGREDIENTS:

500 G READY-ROLLED PUFF PASTRY

PLAIN FLOUR, FOR DUSTING

1 SMALL PACK OF STUFFING

400 G SAUSAGE MEAT OR VEGAN SAUSAGE ROLL MIX

1 EGG, BEATEN

2 TSP NIGELLA OR SESAME SEEDS (OPTIONAL)

EQUIPMENT:

Mixing bowl
Kettle
Measuring jug
Wooden spoon
Knife and fork
Pastry brush
Baking tray
Wire rack

ALLERGY AWARE!
Do not try this where allergies may be an issue.

INSTRUCTIONS:

1. Ask an adult to preheat your oven to 200°C/180°C fan. Lightly dust a surface with flour and roll out your pastry until it is roughly 3 mm thick.

2. Put your sausage meat/mix into a bowl. Ask an adult to boil the kettle and follow the stuffing packet's instructions for how much water should be added. Mix the stuffing up, then add it to your sausage meat/mix and mush it all together with a wooden spoon.

3. Using a fork, scoop out sausage mixture into two long lines across your pastry with roughly 6 cm of pastry either side of the sausage mix. The lines should be the thickness of a fat sausage. Then cut the pastry in between your sausage lines.

4. Carefully fold over one edge of the pastry over the sausage mixture, then use your beaten egg to brush a line along the edge. Fold over the other side of pastry and stick it down with the egg.

5. Cut up the sausage rolls into lengths of 5–10 cm and place them on a lined baking tray.

6. Prick each sausage roll a few times down the middle with a fork, so it cooks inside.

OUCH!

7. Using the rest of your beaten egg, brush the sausage rolls and then sprinkle some nigella or sesame seeds on top, if you'd like to.

8. Now ask an adult to bake them for 30–35 minutes (your pastry will be a lovely golden colour when done). Place your rolls onto a wire rack and leave for about 10 minutes before gobbling them up.

ICE CREAM SUPREME

I scream! You scream! We scream ICE CREAM! Yeti and I are in agreement that there isn't a more perfect food in the world than ice cream. After I have ballet practice and Yeti, well, tries to do ballet – you'll get there, buddy – we like to cool down with a scoop or two – or ten in Yeti's case. What? Ballet is hard! And this ice cream recipe is GOOD!

Ingredients:

200 g dark chocolate, broken into pieces

500 ml double cream

340 g can sweetened condensed milk

1 tsp vanilla extract

3 tbsp organic cocoa powder, sifted

50 g milk chocolate chips

Ice cream cones

ALLERGY AWARE! Do not try this where allergies may be an issue.

Equipment:

Heatproof bowl

Saucepan (or microwave)

Whisk

Freezer-proof container

Instructions:

1 In a heatproof bowl, ask an adult to melt the chocolate over a saucepan of simmering water. Or, if you have one, you can use a microwave instead for this bit – just stir between 30-second bursts until the chocolate is completely melted.

2 Leave the chocolate to cool down a little.

3 Now, in a second bowl, pour the cream, condensed milk and vanilla. Whisk it all together until thickened (about 3 minutes). It's ready when the whisk leaves a trail in the mixture. You don't want it to be too stiff, so take care not to over-whisk.

4 Carefully fold the cocoa powder and melted chocolate into the cream mixture until well combined. Make sure all the chocolate gets mixed in. Chuck in your chocolate chips – keeping a small handful aside – and fold these in too.

5 All of the mixture now needs to go into a 1-litre freezer-proof container. Add the leftover chocolate chips to the top, then cover and freeze for at least 6 hours. You want it to be firm but still scoopable.

CHOC CHIP ICE CREAM

6 Scoop your ice cream into cones or bowls and devour it!

HAP-PEA SHOOTER

SO, YOU THINK YOU'VE GOT GOOD AIM, EH? WELL NOW'S THE TIME TO PUT THAT CLAIM TO THE TEST WITH YOUR OWN PEA SHOOTER. REMEMBER NOT TO AIM AT PEOPLE, ANIMALS OR TEACHERS THOUGH, OR YOU'LL MAKE THEM EXTREMELY UNHAP-PEA.

PEAS

STUFF YOU NEED:

Kitchen roll tube

Sticky tape

Cardboard (you can use a cereal box)

CORNY FLAKES

Scissors

Pencil

Don't forget the peas!

INSTRUCTIONS:

1

Cut a 2 cm strip lengthways out of your kitchen roll tube, then roll the tube to make it thinner, until the inside is about the size of a penny. Use sticky tape to fasten it in place.

2

Now draw a circle on your card or cardboard using a tin, and cut it out. Ask an adult to stab a hole in the centre with a pencil, so that it is big enough to blow through, but small enough that a pea can't get through it. The last thing you want is to inhale the peas!

3

Stick the circle on one end of your tube, using sticky tape to seal the edges. Ask an adult to make sure it is secure.

4

Now inhale, quickly put a frozen pea in the tube and blow! Try setting up some paper cups and see how many you can hit.

GIVE PEAS A CHANCE!

PEAS

DRAW. LAUGH. LOVE.

I ALWAYS CARRY PAPER AND PENS IN MY ART PACK. YOU JUST NEVER KNOW WHEN YOU MIGHT NEED TO SKETCH A QUICK SPIDER TO FREAK OUT YOUR TEACHER WITH OR WHIP UP A POSTER FOR THAT BORING BIT OF WALL BY THE LIBRARY. ANOTHER THING IT'S HANDY FOR IS PLAYING PICTURE CONSEQUENCES WITH MY MATES, RUBI AND DENNIS. ONCE WE MANAGED TO COME UP WITH A CHARACTER WHO LOOKED EXACTLY LIKE BIGGY SMELLS, THE LIBRARIAN, SO WE FRAMED IT AND GAVE IT TO THEM – THEY WERE THRILLED!

STUFF YOU NEED:

Pencils

Paper

1–2 friends

INSTRUCTIONS:

URGH! SOMEONE HASN'T BRUSHED THEIR TEETH!

1. Everyone needs to start by drawing a head at the top of their own piece of paper.

2. Add a neck and fold the paper over, so that the two lines are just showing and the head is hidden from sight. Pass it to your neighbour (friend next to you, not your neighbour next door – they might be confused). No peeking!

3. Now everyone draws a torso. Fold the paper over again, leaving just two tiny bits of lines visible and pass to your friend. Next, draw some legs and fold it over again. Then lastly, all draw some crazy feet.

4. Pass your drawings around once more and take it in turns to unfold them to discover your bonkers creations!

NOW THAT'S A GREAT LOOK!

59

GET ANIMATED!

When I'm not posting videos of my life on You-Hoo, or filming my teachers sneakily farting and picking their noses, I like to create epic stop-motion films. Sometimes I get Plug to help me out, but he gets a bit bored and wanders off halfway through, so I mainly create blamazing scenes using my action figures or other toys.

Stuff you need:

BEANO

DENNIS MENACE ACTION TOY

Action toys or a friend

12:35

Smartphone camera

Stop-motion app

Instructions:

Why not design your own film set using a cereal box?

1. Set up your scene and think about what you'd like to happen. Position your phone so that it won't move and all shots are from the same angle.

2. Take a photo.

3. Make a small change to your scene. How much you move things depends on how big your subject is. If you're filming a person, they can move a centimetre or two per image, but if you're filming small toys, you'll want to move them only a tiny bit per picture.

4. Take a photo.

5. Make another small change.

6. Take another photo.

7. Keep following this pattern until you've finished your story.

8. You'll need to download a free stop-motion app (ask an adult for help if you need to). This will allow you to put all your photos together and create an awesome video. Or you can use Windows Movie Maker or a different type of video-editing software.

03:25

⚠ If you are using an action figure, then make sure it has moveable joints. And remember to keep your camera or phone still, otherwise your film will look like it's in the middle of an earthquake!

Stick in the Spud

Potatoes are a seriously under-appreciated vegetable! And they are brilliant for getting arty with because not only can they make lots of cool designs, but they are compostable afterwards – spud-tacular! I've made some epic Halloween and Christmas decorations for Dennis's treehouse before, and am planning some cool banners for the 'Pretty Awesome Race in the Park' (P.A.R.P.) this year too.

STUFF YOU NEED:

Knife (ask an adult) ⚠

Pencil

Potato

Paints

Tracing paper
(can use baking paper instead)

INSTRUCTIONS:

1

⚠️

Ask an adult to cut your potato in half. Cut it halfway along the long edge as this will give you more potato to hold onto when you're stamping.

2

On tracing paper, draw around your potato, and use this to make your design the right size. Remember that whatever you don't cut out is what will stamp, so plan your stamp in reverse.

3

Once you've planned your design, place it on the flesh face of your potato half and then use a sharp pencil to go over your design, leaving an indent in the potato.

4 ⚠️

Then ask a grown-up to cut out your design for you.

5

Dip your potato in paint and stamp it on your paper wherever you like. Wash it off under cold water and pat dry with kitchen roll if you want to change the colour of your paint.

THE PLOT THICKENS!

YETI LOVE STORIES. YETI WORK IN BEANOTOWN LIBRARY. YETI READ ALMOST ALL BOOKS THERE, SO BETTY COME UP WITH GAME BEFORE I RUN OUT OF BOOKS TO READ! YETI AND BETTY WRITE OWN BOOKS! THEY MUCH FUNNIER, BUT NOT ALWAYS MAKE SENSE . . . CAN YOU TRY?

STUFF YOU NEED:

- Paper
- Pens or pencils
- 2 or more friends

INSTRUCTIONS:

This is similar to Sketch's drawing game on page 58, but this time you are writing sections of a story.

1. Everyone playing writes a sentence that introduces their first character and leaves the sentence open for your friend to add a second. For example, you could write:

> Once upon a time, Princess Fartsalot was out for a stroll when she met...

Write the last word (in this instance, 'met') on a new line.

> met...

2. Fold back your piece of paper to hide your sentence, but leave the last word on show, so the next person knows where to pick up. Swap with your friend.

3. Now the next person gets to come up with a second character. They then get to start a new sentence about what happens, leaving it open with a connecting word: and, then, because, therefore, etc. Always make sure to put that last word on a new line. So for instance, you could write:

> met...
> ... a talking dragon called Bruce. 'I will eat you now,' said Bruce, then...

4. If you're playing with more than two people, you'd now pass on and the next person would introduce another character, until each person has added a character to the story. Once you've all added a character to each other's stories (try to come up with a different one for each), it's now time to switch back to your original story and write another sentence for your character.

5. Keep writing sentences and ending them on connecting words, switching stories as you go.

6. When you've switched it a few times, pass it to your friend for the final time and then take it in turns to read the stories aloud. You'll never read another story like it!

A WHEELY GOOD DECODER

MESSAGE:

Being a secret agent . . .
I mean . . . an ordinary
boy living in Beanotown,
I like to play football
with my best friends Dennis
and Mandi, cracking the
odd secret code and making
things. And before you
ask, I choose to wear a
tuxedo every day because
it has very useful pockets
for things that aren't
spy gadgets or anything
remotely spy related, OK?
I use this spy decoder
wheel to communicate
secretly with my . . .
er . . . sister.

FOR YOUR EYES ONLY

STUFF YOU NEED:

- A4 card
- Pencil
- Scissors
- Ruler
- Pen
- Paper fastener

0 1 2 3 4 5 6 7 8 9 10

INSTRUCTIONS:

1. Draw a large 13 cm-wide circle in the corner of your card, and cut it out.

2. With a pencil and ruler, mark the centre of your circle, then around the outside, make marks every 1.5 cm. Use a ruler and a thin pen to draw a line from the centre to each mark around the outside, which should leave you with 27 segments.

3. Now draw another circle, this time 9 cm wide and do the same, making marks around the outside every 1 cm.

4. Fill in the alphabet around the edges of your circles, one letter in each segment, then pop a question mark in the final space. If you want to make your code REALLY hard to break, then mix up the alphabet on your inner circle.

5. Ask an adult to stab a hole in the centre of each of your circles with a sharp pencil. Put your paper fastener through both circles, with the smaller one on top.

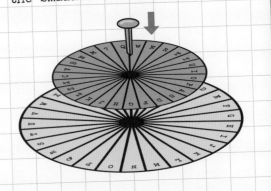

6. Now you've got your code, you can spin your decoder wheel around, settle on a position with the letters lined up, then write your top-secret code. For your recipient to decode it, just give them which inner letter lines up with the outside A. Without that key, it would take someone AGES to work out your message!

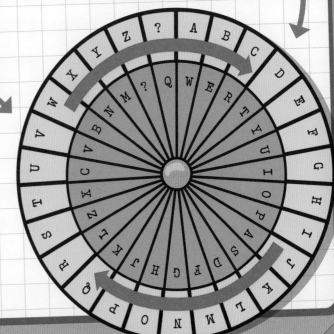

Instrument Until Proven Guilty

Elastic Band Guitar / Lolly Stick Harmonica (By Freddie Brown)

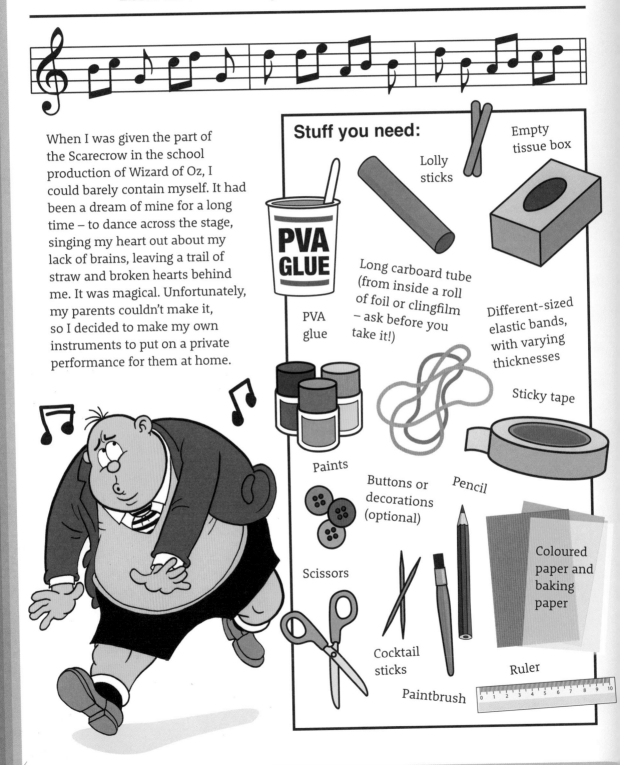

When I was given the part of the Scarecrow in the school production of Wizard of Oz, I could barely contain myself. It had been a dream of mine for a long time – to dance across the stage, singing my heart out about my lack of brains, leaving a trail of straw and broken hearts behind me. It was magical. Unfortunately, my parents couldn't make it, so I decided to make my own instruments to put on a private performance for them at home.

Stuff you need:

- Lolly sticks
- Empty tissue box
- PVA glue
- Long carboard tube (from inside a roll of foil or clingfilm – ask before you take it!)
- Different-sized elastic bands, with varying thicknesses
- Sticky tape
- Paints
- Buttons or decorations (optional)
- Pencil
- Scissors
- Cocktail sticks
- Paintbrush
- Coloured paper and baking paper
- Ruler

Elastic Guitar:

1 Put the end of the cardboard tube up against the end of your tissue box. Draw around the tube and cut out a hole in the box – you can always ask an adult to help with this part. Paint the tube and lolly sticks, and leave to dry.

2 Take off any plastic or extra paper on the tissue box and open it out flat. Paint inside it and leave to dry. Cut out some coloured paper and stick it down to the base of the box (this will show on the inside of the guitar).

3 Now, with the painted side on the outside, glue the box back together again. Leave to dry. Feed the carboard tube into the hole you made earlier, then secure it firmly in place with some sticky tape.

4 The lolly sticks now need to be glued at each end of the oval hole in the front of the tissue box. Leave to dry. Next, carefully stretch the elastic bands around the whole box.

5 Now you can decorate your guitar using buttons, sequins, pom-poms, Grandpa's false teeth* – anything you fancy!

*Maybe ask him first though!

Lolly Stick Harmonica:

1 Take two lolly sticks and paint them on both sides. Leave to dry.

2 Now, cut some baking paper to the width and length of the lolly sticks.

3 Take your cocktail stick and cut it into two 2-cm pieces, removing the sharp ends.

4 Layer up your elements, placing one lolly stick, then the baking paper, then a cocktail stick across at each end, then the other lolly stick on top. Secure both ends around the cocktail sticks with rubber bands. It's now ready for you to blow through the gap in the middle!

FREDDIE ROCKS!

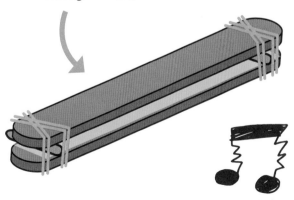

NEW KID ON THE SOCK

NO ONE LIKES DRESSING UP MORE THAN I DO, WHICH MEANS SOMETIMES I HAVE TO DO IT ALONE. PUTTING ON A ONE-MAN PLAY CAN BE EXHAUSTING – AND DIZZYING – PLAYING ALL THE PARTS. IT'S MUCH EASIER PUTTING ON A SOCK-PUPPET SHOW. JUST WHATEVER YOU DO – DON'T USE DENNIS'S SOCKS – THEY STINK!

STUFF YOU NEED:

Pom-poms

PVA glue

Cereal box

Googly eyes or buttons

Scissors

A clean sock

Felt

INSTRUCTIONS:

1 First, turn your sock inside-out and spread it out on a flat surface, with the heel pointing upwards.

2 Grab a cereal box and cut a rectangle the same width as your sock and at least 5 cm long – the longer you cut it, the deeper your mouth will be.

4 Use some felt to cut out a long semi-circle for the tongue, about the width of your puppet's mouth. Add a line of glue along the straight edge and stick it into the back of the mouth.

3 Fold your cardboard rectangle in half and coat the inside with glue. Clamp this down onto the toe end of your sock and leave to dry. Turn your sock outside-in and there you'll see your mouth! The heel will be the top of your puppet's head.

5 Now glue two pom-poms for eyes on top of the head and add some buttons or googly eyes. Add another button or small pom-pom for the puppet's nose. Customise however you like!

6

Give your puppet a name! What about Dwayne 'The Sock' Johnson? Or even Meryl Feet?

A FLIPPING GOOD TIME

LAST WEEK, JEM DID THIS TOTALLY BLAMAZING BMX STUNT IN THE BEANOTOWN SKATEPARK. SHE SPED DOWN THE RAMP AT LIKE A MILLION MILES AN HOUR AND FLIPPED HERSELF ROUND IN THIS TOTALLY EPIC MOVE. IT WAS SERIOUSLY COOL! I RECORDED THE MOVE IN A FLIP BOOK, SO I COULD SHOW DENNIS LATER. IT WORKED A TREAT.

STUFF YOU'LL NEED:

Pen or pencil

Stack of lightweight paper

INSTRUCTIONS:

1 You're going to need a stack of lightweight paper (stapled or clipped together), a pad of sticky notes or a small paperback notebook – something that's easy to flip through. The paper should be about 10 cm x 10 cm, but don't worry if it's slightly bigger or smaller.

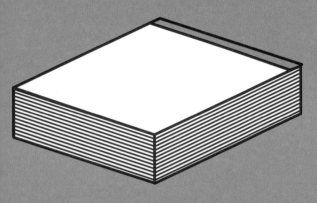

2 On the last sheet of paper in your notebook or stack, draw your first picture (in pencil first, then go over in pen later). This will be the first image in your sequence. Draw it towards the bottom right–hand corner, so it's easily seen when flipped.

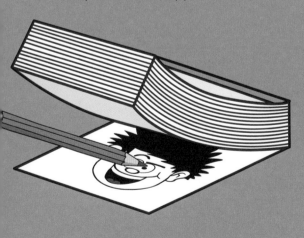

3 On your next sheet of paper, draw a slight variation of the same image. So, for example, if you're drawing a stick figure waving their hand, keep the body in the same place, but change where the arm is to give the effect of movement. To help keep your images in the same place, you can hold your paper against a window to see the drawing below.

4 Keep going, drawing slightly different images on top of the last image you drew.

5 Once you've finished, get flipping! To do this effectively, put your thumb on the bottom–right edge of your notebook and pull it upwards slowly. You don't want to skip any pages, so make sure none of the pages are sticking together, then practise getting the right flipping speed.

To make your animation a little more interesting, add some colour. Just remember to use the same colours on each page, to keep the image consistent for flipping through.

OUTDOOR ADVENTURES

THE WILDERNESS AWAITS! (WELL, YOUR GARDEN OR LOCAL PARK DOES AT LEAST.) WHETHER YOU'VE GOT A FRIEND OVER, OR HAVE SOME TIME ON YOUR OWN, THERE'S LOADS OF FUN STUFF FOR YOU TO GET UP TO OUTSIDE. SO, WHAT ARE YOU WAITING FOR? TURN THE PAGE AND GET STARTED!

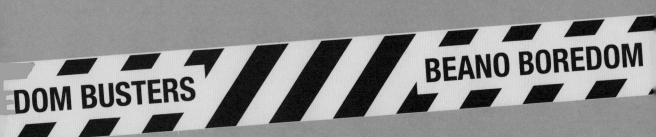

COME ON, DEN

Take a look under there. Under where? Ha! I made you say underwear! Making a den is always a blam way to spend your time. Drag your parents or grown-ups away from their Starbutts coffee and get them to help you build an epic base for plotting your next pranks in.

INSTRUCTIONS:

1 Enlist an adult to help – and make them do all the heavy lifting, so you don't have to! You're going to need a flat bit of ground in your garden or nearby woods to build your den on.

DEN-TASTIC AREA

✔

✗

2 Look for a knobbly structure - not grandparents, they never stay still for long enough! A great one is to find a living tree that has a thick, sturdy horizontal branch about head height (avoid dead trees). You can use the branch as a ceiling support. Other natural structures also work, but make sure they aren't near any hollows that look like an animal might live in there.

3 Get hunting for some solid branches. You don't want them to be too heavy though because they might hurt someone. If you struggle to find many of these, then ask an adult if you can borrow broom handles or some light-weight chairs from home.

Don't break off living branches - always respect nature.

4 You need a strong frame for your den structure. A leaning tree or sturdy tree branch is great for this, but you can also wedge three branches together to form a triangle and make a circular den by adding more branches, one at a time. You can also make a tent shape by leaning branches against each other. Put a branch across the top and use rope or strong string to tie them together along its length (see page 24 for knots). You'll need some help for this one, unless you have extra arms you can whip out. If you're in your garden, ask an adult for an old bed sheet or blanket to drape over your structure.

5 Finish off your den by putting a picnic blanket and some old cushions inside, as well as a supply of delicious snacks to fuel your plotting.

It Wouldn't Bee Home Without You

BEE KIND!

BEE AMAZING!

RIGHT HONEYS, WE NEED TO TAKE CARE OF OUR ANIMALS AND WILDLIFE. SUPERHEROES WON'T SAVE THE PLANET – WE HAVE TO DO IT OURSELVES! AND BEES ARE PARTICULARLY AWESOME LITTLE CREATURES THAT REALLY NEED PROTECTING. SO LET'S ALL BEE ENVIRONMENTALLY AWARE AND GET HELPING OUR BEE-UTIFUL PLANET.

BEE AN ECO-WARRIOR!

Stuff you need:

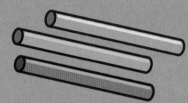

Tubes (paper straws or rolled cereal boxes)

A mug (pick an old and unwanted one!)

String

Scissors

Instructions:

1 Cut all your tubes or straws so that they are just a little bit shorter than the length of the mug. This is to protect them from rain.

2 Pack the tubes or straws in tightly so that they don't fall out. If you'd prefer, you could cover the front with some wire mesh large enough to let the bees in, but small enough to keep the straws in place.

BEES LOVE TEA!

3 Tie some string securely around the handle of your mug, then find a spot to hang it up outside. Your bee hotel needs to be in a sheltered area, about 1–2 metres above the ground. In a tree, facing north–east is a good place (you want it to get the morning sun). Ask an adult to hang it up for you.

BEES LOVE TEA!

I'M ROOTING FOR YOU

As you probably know, Paul the Potato is one of my best friends. He's like a brother to me. But get this: some people eat their potato pals! There have even been a couple of close calls when my parents have tried to eat Paul! If the worst happens and someone eats your veggie friend, don't lose all hope: you might be able grow them back!

" "
...

STUFF YOU NEED:

Compost

Potato peelings

Carrot tops

MULTI-PURPOSE COMPOST

Potato grow bag or deep container

Plant pot, 35-45 cm deep

Old tub

PAUL THE POTATO

1 Fill a potato grow bag with about 50 litres (one big bag) of compost. Potatoes grow best between March and May.

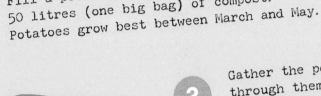

2 Gather the potato peelings and riffle through them until you find pieces with eyes on them — those are the little sprout bits. Keep these and chuck out the rest of the peelings.

3 Dry the peelings overnight, then plant them in the potato bag with the eyes facing upwards. With any luck, your peelings will sprout and you'll eventually have many new friends to choose from!

CARRIE THE CARROT

1 The best time to plant yourself a carrot buddy is from April to July. Take the tops of your fallen friends and pop them in a shallow container of water.

2 Place on a windowsill until your carrot tops begin to sprout roots.

3 Fill your plant pot with compost, leaving a small gap at the top. Bury your carrot tops with the green leaves just poking out the top of the soil.

4 The leaves will then grow and flower, giving you seeds to then plant and grow fresh carrot friends from. When the carrots are finally ready to harvest, you'll see the orange tops sitting above the soil.

A MO-MINT-OUS OCCASION

Looking for an explosive time? Everyone knows I love a good science experiment, and if it happens to explode, then even better. Dennis actually fell over when I showed him this one, and Pie Face squealed so loudly that Rasher the pig came running to save him!

STUFF YOU NEED:

Mints

Widl
Diet Cola

- Sticky tape
- Scissors
- Pack of mint sweets
- 2 litre bottle of diet cola, room temperature
- Old clothes (you're going to get sticky!)
- Protective goggles
- Outside space

INSTRUCTIONS:

1 Cut yourself a long strip of sticky tape, about the length of a ruler, and place it sticky side up on a surface.

2 Grab your mint sweets and line as many of them as you can along half of your sticky tape.

(Maybe eat one before, just to test they are indeed mints!)

4 Now take your cola and mints outside and check with an adult where's best to conduct your experiment – it's probably best NOT to do this right next to your grandma while she's napping!

3 Fold over your tape to cover the top of your mints. This will allow you to drop loads of them in your cola at the same time, making a huge fizzy explosion.

5 Take the lid off your cola bottle and dangle your mint strip above the opening. When you're ready, drop your mints in and dodge the blast!

6 RUN!

BOOM!

Widl Diet Cola

And finally . . . clean up your mess afterwards! Litter bugs aren't cool.

Widl Diet Cola

FEED THE BIRDS

Animals are awesome things and I keep as many as I can. But Patrick the pigeon is my total BFF. We love sitting outside, bird watching together. In fact, one day I was so distracted by a long-tailed tit that I started snacking on Wiggy the dog's kibble instead of my crisps. It was quite nice, actually! A great way to bring birds to your garden is by building a bird feeder.

Sidney
(Sidicus Sillicus)

Patrick*
(Pigeonus Pattius)

*Patrick is not a giant pigeon.

Drawing pin

Pencils

30 cm string

Widl BIRD SEED

Scissors

Plastic bottle

Bird seed

INSTRUCTIONS:

You're going to want an adult's help with this activity as things can get fiddly and sharp. Tell them it's for cute birds – no one can say no to cute birds, can they? ⚠️

1. Grab yourself an empty plastic bottle with a lid, then take the labels off, wash it out thoroughly and leave it to dry. If the bottle isn't fully dry, then the bird feed will go mouldy – bleurgh!

2. Using a drawing pin, carefully make two holes near the bottom of your bottle. The holes need to be opposite each other and you'll need to press the pin in hard to puncture the plastic. Ask an adult if you're struggling.

3. Get your scissors and carefully make your holes a bit bigger. You do this by pushing the tip of the scissors through the hole and twisting. The holes need to be the right size for a pencil to go through, but not too big, otherwise it will just fall out.

4. Push your pencil through your newly made holes. You now have your first perch! Ensure that the same amount of the pencil is sticking out both sides, so the feeder is balanced. You don't want cross, wonky birds!

5. Add another perch or two farther up your bottle, using the same method as before, with 10 cm in between each pencil. Make sure to pop your pencils through different sides of the bottle, so that they cross over each other.

6. You now need to make the feeding holes, so your birds can reach the seeds. About 5 cm above each perch, make more holes with your pin and scissors. They need to be big enough for the birds to get to the feed, but small enough to keep the birdseed in.

7. At the top of your bottle, on the neck, make holes facing each other using your drawing pin. Widen these holes a little with your scissors. This is what you'll use to hang your bottle up. If you're using a large bottle, then make four holes, so extra string can be used for more strength. Feed your string through the holes and tie the ends firmly together in a knot.

8. Now you can fill up your bottle with the birdseed (make sure you use mixes or seeds that are for smaller birds, such as blue tits and sparrows). The bottle doesn't need to be completely filled, just make sure the feeding holes are covered. Remember to replace the bottle cap, so that birds don't get their little heads stuck in the top. Now find a medium-height tree branch or pole and hang your feeder up. If you don't have a garden, then these work really well hanging outside a window too.

GET A HEAD!

Stuff you need:

An old pair of tights

Potting mixture

POTTING MIXTURE

I happen to be good at everything, just ask Mr Teacher. It's just something I was born with; it's called perfection. Last week I made a brilliant grass head that looked exactly like Mr Teacher. I left it on his desk, and I could tell from his expression that he adored it.

GRASS SEED

Grass seed*

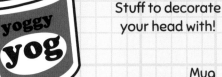

Stuff to decorate your head with!

yoggy yog

Yogurt pot

Mug

TEACHER'S PET

Scissors

*YOU CAN ALSO USE CRESS SEEDS. THEN YOU CAN EAT IT TOO!

86

Instructions:

1 Take the tights or stocking and cut off a section, roughly 20 cm up from the toe area. If your tights are missing their toes – perhaps someone beat you to it – then you can tie a knot in the tights and turn them inside out to hide it. Grab a mug and stretch your piece of tights over it, with the toe section dangling inside the mug.

2 This bit can get messy, so it's probably best to do it outside if you can. Pour two teaspoons of grass seed in the bottom, then fill the rest of the mug with your sawdust or potting mix.

3 Tie a knot in your tights, as close as you can to the inside mix, and squish it into a ball.

4 Now it's time to shape it into a face. Position the ball so the knot is at the bottom and on one side, pinch a piece of the tights with a bit of sawdust/potting mix inside and twist it to create a nose. Use a piece of thread to secure it – you might want to ask an adult for help. Next, let's add the details. Grab your yogurt pot and decorate it to look like a torso. Then pop your head on top and glue on some googly eyes and a mouth.

SNIP
SNIP

5 Dunk the head you have just made in a bowl of water and also fill the yogurt pot about half full, making sure the tights are dangling in the water underneath the head. Then wait a week and your head will have grown a fine mop of hair! You can trim it into funky styles and it will grow back.

LESS TALK, MORE CHALK

EVERYONE KNOWS I'M THE LEADER OF THE BASH STREET KIDS, AND IF ANYONE DARES TO FORGET IT, THEN I JUST REMIND THEM WITH AN EPIC PRANK!

LAST WEEK, I PULLED THE BEST PRANK OUTSIDE BASH STREET TOWERS. WITH THE HELP OF SKETCH KHAD, WE USED PAVEMENT CHALK TO MAKE IT LOOK AS THOUGH THERE WAS A HOLE IN THE FLOOR. PEOPLE WERE JUMPING OUT OF THEIR SKINS WHEN THEY SAW IT!

STUFF YOU NEED:

Pavement chalk

Old cloth

INSTRUCTIONS:

Find a spot on the pavement where you're allowed to draw, then get out your chalks and start drawing a hole. First, draw the edge of the hole, then use your colours to make it look like it extends down into the depths. Use your cloth to blend your lines to make it look even more realistic.

THAT'S NOT ALL THE FUN TO HAVE WITH PAVEMENT CHALK! HERE ARE SOME MORE IDEAS:

Use your driveway or front garden to draw a maze from your front door to the street!

Use a pathway to draw a bunch of fun instructions for people to complete to pass, such as hop like a frog, twirl like a ballerina or fart like a cow.

hop like a frog!

Use your driveway or patio to draw a classic boardgame but HUGE, where you're the playing pieces!

FINISH

START

64	63	62	61	60	59	58	57
49	50	51	52	53	54	55	56
48	47	46	45	44	43	42	41
33	34	35	36	37	38	39	40
32	31	30	29	28	27	26	25
17	18	19	20	21	22	23	24
16	15	14	13	12	11	10	9
1	2	3	4	5	6	7	8

Scavenger Found it Yet?

Vito and I like to go on adventures to find creepy crawlies and other animals in the woods around Lake Mess. We hunt around in the soil, climb a few trees and often get stuck in rabbit holes, but it's all good fun. And we always meet a new animal or insect to make friends with!

Camera

Stopwatch

0:00

Pen or pencil

INSTRUCTIONS:

1. For this scavenger hunt, you're going to need to be outside with nature, so try to get to a park, woods or garden, and always tell a groan-up where you're going – or drag one along with you.

2. Now, look at the table below – these are the things you need to find. When you spot one of them, take a photo or just tick it off your list (no cheating)!

3. Set yourself an hour and see how many of the things you can spot in that time. If you manage to find all of them, then shout 'Blamazing' as loudly as you can! Better yet, grab some friends and make it a competition to see who can find everything first.

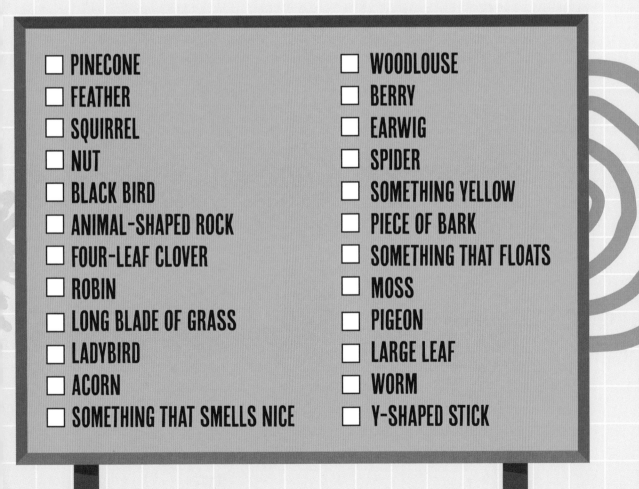

- ☐ PINECONE
- ☐ FEATHER
- ☐ SQUIRREL
- ☐ NUT
- ☐ BLACK BIRD
- ☐ ANIMAL-SHAPED ROCK
- ☐ FOUR-LEAF CLOVER
- ☐ ROBIN
- ☐ LONG BLADE OF GRASS
- ☐ LADYBIRD
- ☐ ACORN
- ☐ SOMETHING THAT SMELLS NICE
- ☐ WOODLOUSE
- ☐ BERRY
- ☐ EARWIG
- ☐ SPIDER
- ☐ SOMETHING YELLOW
- ☐ PIECE OF BARK
- ☐ SOMETHING THAT FLOATS
- ☐ MOSS
- ☐ PIGEON
- ☐ LARGE LEAF
- ☐ WORM
- ☐ Y-SHAPED STICK

SCAVENGER PIGEONS

I tried to set up a scavenger hunt for Peeps the dog, by hiding my twin brother Sidney in Beanotown Zoo. But apparently the apes kept flinging their poo at him, so he said he wouldn't play anymore. Would have made it more smell-ventful, but whatevs! Anyway, here is a scavenger hunt for about the town. Stevie is going to film us hunting for it all!

STUFF YOU NEED:

Stopwatch

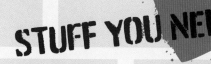

Pen or pencil

Camera
(or a phone
with a camera)

GRRRR!

INSTRUCTIONS:

1. Unlike the previous scavenger hunt, this one is for a city or town, so you'll definitely need an adult with you.

2. Just like before, bring your camera along to take pictures of the things you spot or tick them off the list as you find them.

3. Set yourself a certain amount of time – an hour is always good – and see how many items you can find before the time's up. If you get them all, shout 'Pants' really loudly.

- ☐ Lamppost
- ☐ Something blue
- ☐ Storefront awning
- ☐ Poster
- ☐ Apple
- ☐ Dustbin
- ☐ Traffic warden
- ☐ Scooter
- ☐ Seagull
- ☐ A straw
- ☐ Something round
- ☐ Police car
- ☐ Pigeon
- ☐ Post box
- ☐ Café
- ☐ Graffiti
- ☐ Yellow car
- ☐ Phone box
- ☐ Dog
- ☐ Flower
- ☐ Motorbike
- ☐ Zebra crossing
- ☐ Shopping trolley
- ☐ Tree

KEEP IT UP

BEING PART OF BEANOTOWN UNTIED FOOTBALL TEAM IS TOTALLY EPIC, BUT I DIDN'T GET TO BE WHERE I AM TODAY BY SITTING ON MY GRASS. SKILLS TAKE TIME AND DEDICATION TO MASTER, SO I'M GOING TO GIVE YOU SOME GOAL-DEN TIPS ON HOW TO DO KEEPIE-UPPIES THAT WILL LEAVE YOUR OPPOSITION DRIBBLING.

INSTRUCTIONS:

1 In order to get really good at these, you need to perfect the basics first. So begin by bouncing the ball on the flat surface of your thigh (not anywhere on your knee, or on anyone else's thigh – they might object). Bounce it once and then catch it. Keep doing this until you feel confident that you've mastered it.

2 Now we're going to move to your dominant foot (the one you naturally lead with). You want the ball to bounce where your toes start, so keep your toes slightly pointed up to stop the ball going forward. The ball needs to go straight up. Like before, bounce it on your foot once, then catch it. Keep practising until you feel you can do more than one kick at a time.

3 It's time for your other foot. You'll find that the best players are really strong using both feet for keepie-uppies, so it's worth putting the practise in.

4 Practise kicking the ball between different parts of your body until it starts to feel natural. Then keep practising! By doing it every day, your legs will get stronger and your muscle memory for each motion will improve.

KEEP IT UP AND YOU'LL SOON BE JUGGLING THE BALL LIKE A PRO!

Thinking A-cloud

Sometimes I give myself headaches by frowning too much. Do you ever do that? To relax, I like to take my pet rabbit Milo out into the garden and we lie on the grass and watch the clouds. I use the shapes to come up with stories in which I'm every bit as daring as I'd love to be in real life. For instance, I once saw a pig in a top hat, who became Lord Snotter, the evil master villain that Princess Candoattitude vanquished to save her people.

1

Find a quiet spot to lie on the ground. If you don't have grass, then take a couple of cushions with you, so you're comfortable.

2 Begin by just thinking about your breathing. Take nice slow breaths in, and with every exhale imagine releasing any tension you're holding in your tummy or chest. Start to notice your limbs relaxing and your back resting into the ground or cushion. Relax your neck and let your shoulders drop.

WISPY

3 Now take a look up at the sky. The clouds above us can form many different shapes, each one unique, each one beautiful. Some are fluffy, floaty and wispy, while others are rolling, misty, dense and stormy. But all offer scope for the imagination.

FLUFFY

STORMY

BAA!

4 Look for recognisable shapes for inspiration. You might find characters, props or even landscapes up in the clouds. The longer you look, the more you'll see, and before long, you'll have spotted enough things to base a story on. If you're struggling for inspiration in the sky, then look around you on the ground. Ideas are everywhere.

5 Now come up with a story! You don't need to write it down, and it doesn't need to be long or particularly complicated. It can even be a joke. Or you can just watch how the scene unfolds up in the sky as the clouds move. Just relax and enjoy yourself!

ORGANISED MAYHEM

GRAB A SIBLING, A FRIEND OR EVEN AN ADULT OR TWO, AND LET'S PLAY SOME GAMES! WHETHER IT'S SUNNY OR CHUCKING IT DOWN OUTSIDE, WE'VE GOT YOU COVERED FOR CHAOTIC AND HILARIOUS THINGS TO DO TOGETHER IN THIS CHAPTER.

Penny Hunters

My son Dennis is a genius, but he can be very naughty. Just this morning, he stapled the bottoms of my trousers together, so my feet wouldn't go through. It was really irritating. I didn't even know we had a stapler – I thought we were a paperclip family! He's worst when he's bored though, so sometimes I set him off on a penny hunt to keep him occupied . . .

PARP!

Stuff you need:

100 pennies

Instructions:

This is the easiest activity in the world. All you need to do is hide 100 pennies all over the house and garden. Make sure they are in tricky-to-spot places though. Then set your mates off on a hunt to find them all. The person who finds the most, wins. Simples!

STUCK IN THE MUD

I love this game! Tagging my friends is great practice for when I'm hunting down ghosts and ghouls!

YOU WILL NEED:
A bunch of players – the more the merrier!

INSTRUCTIONS:

1. The rules of this game are simple. Choose one person to be It. As It, it's your job to tag everyone.

2. Everyone else will be working as a team. If you are tagged, you are then 'stuck in the mud' and have to stand still with your legs wide and your arms out.

3. To free a player who's 'stuck', you have to crawl through their legs – or if it's wet outside, just high-five both of their hands. While you are freeing someone, you are immune from being tagged.

4. The game ends when everyone is 'stuck in the mud'. How quickly can you finish the game as It?

CAPTURE THE FLAG

CAN'T STOP FOR LONG, I'VE GOT PLACES TO GO AT VERY HIGH SPEEDS, BUT AS I'M PASSING, I THOUGHT I'D CHUCK YOU A COOL GAME TO PLAY — CAPTURE THE FLAG. MY BFFS MINNIE, DENNIS, ROGER AND I PLAY THIS A LOT, THOUGH THEY CAN NEVER CATCH ME. I'M ALWAYS THE FIRST TO GET TO THE FLAG, BUT OFTEN SKID STRAIGHT PAST IT! AND ONCE, I WAS RUNNING SO FAST WITH THE FLAG THAT IT CAUGHT FIRE!

STUFF YOU NEED:

2 hand towels or T-shirts
(if you don't have flags)

Minimum of 3 eagle-eyed, quick-witted friends

BEANO

INSTRUCTIONS:

JAIL

TEAM A AREA

1 Split up into two teams and decide on your play-area boundaries. You'll need to separate the zones for each team, so you might find it easier to choose someone to do this (stops arguments!).

2 Pick what's going to be your 'Jail'. A tree or something similar works well.

3 Now each team needs to hide their flag (or towel) within their zone.

4 Your challenge is to find the other team's flag and get it back into your own zone, while tagging the other team's members.

5 If you are tagged when you are in the other team's zone, then it's off to jail for you! You can only be set free by one of your teammates tagging you.

6 How many times will you get sent to the slammer? There are no limits, so run like the wind!

TEAM B AREA

JAIL

ESCAPE ROOM

WHEN I'M NOT PRANKING MY FRIENDS OR LEAVING FAKE FINGERS IN MY PARENTS' TEA, I LIKE TO CREATE PUZZLES FOR PEOPLE. A GREAT WAY TO EXPLORE LOTS OF DIFFERENT CHALLENGES AND TASKS IS TO SET UP AN ESCAPE ROOM GAME. I FILMED HEENA ONCE TRYING TO CRACK THE CODES TO UNLOCK HER BEDROOM DOOR. SHE WAS STUCK IN THERE FOR HOURS!

1

Pick a room (or rooms) to hold the game in. It needs to be a large enough space for your players to move around in, and also big enough for any props and clues you want to use.

2

Choose a theme. This adds a story to your game and links each activity together. You could set up a Sherlock Holmes theme, a haunted-house scenario or base it on a favourite book - let your imagination run wild!

3

Set a time limit. If this is your first escape room, then it's a good idea to set a 30-minute time frame.

0:00

Lamp

Fireplace

Armchair

Rug
(you can hide things under this)

Sofa
(so good!)

Window

Beano comics (essential reading!)

Telly

Door

Book case (books are perfect for hiding clues)

Window

7

Work on your poker face as you watch your friends puzzle their way through your story. Be ready with some hints in case players get stuck, but don't give away too much.

6

Set some rules for your friends at the beginning - no mobile phones for looking up the answers and don't touch mum's expensive vase, for example!

4

Write a storyline for your game. This will give your escape room a purpose, but don't make it too complicated, or you might lose your friends for weeks. It could be something like there is treasure hidden, and only by cracking the codes and solving the puzzles will you be able to get to it. Or perhaps there's a stink bomb that needs diffusing. Get creative!

MEGA STINK BOMB

5

Now break up the storyline, so it's in sections. Each section should have its own puzzle or code to crack and leads into the next one, until you achieve the overall goal. So if your players need to unlock the room they are in, you could hide clues in a sequence that will lead to where the key is hidden.

FORTY FORTY

Becoming an expert ghost hunter doesn't happen overnight. You need to be fit and have keen senses, which both take practise. One of the games I love to play with my friends to work on my hunting skills is called Forty Forty. It's great because it combines all my fave things – teamwork, stealth, wits and lots of giggles. So read up on the rules and catch me if you can!

STUFF YOU NEED:

2 or more friends

A big space with hiding spots – small woods or park

Snacks (OK, so not technically needed, but always appreciated!)

CRISPOS!

CHOCCO

26
27
28

INSTRUCTIONS:

1 Pick someone to be It and somewhere that's going to be your base, such as a tree or lamppost.

2 It needs to close their eyes and count to 40 out loud while the other players run off and hide nearby.

3 The aim is for the players to get to the base without It seeing them (this is a spotting game, not a tagging game). If It does spot a player, they must run back to the base and shout,

'FORTY FORTY I SEE (NAME)!'

The person who's been seen then has to return to the base and wait for the game to end.

4 The winner is the first person who is able to get to the base without being seen, and shouts . . .

'FORTY FORTY HOME!'

5 The first person who was spotted at the start of the game then becomes It for the next one. Or if no one was spotted, then it's the last person to reach the base.

GNASHER LOVES LAMPPOSTS!

Shipwreck

ALL ABOARD MY SHIP! IN THIS GAME, I AM THE CAPTAIN AND YOU MUST DO EVERYTHING I SAY, OR YOU'RE OUT!

Stuff you need:

A bunch of crewmates

A big open space – indoors or outdoors

Instructions:

1 First you need to choose a captain of the ship (me, duh!).

2 Then that captain needs to tell everyone which end of the area is the 'bow' of the ship and which end is the 'stern'. They'll also designate a 'brig'– an area to the side of the main game, where players go when they're out.

3 The captain will then call out a bunch of commands, and the last person to follow them each time gets sent to the brig. Whoever is last standing wins!

The commands:

Roll call
The crew must line up in the middle of the area, snap their feet together, salute and shout, 'Aye–aye Captain!'

Climb the rigging
Everyone must act as though they are climbing a ladder.

Drop anchor
Crewmates drop to the floor and spread out in their best impression of an anchor.

Aargh, pirates!
All players cover one eye, hold up a hooked finger and hobble around, shouting 'Aargh!' in their best impersonation of a pirate. The player with the worst impression goes to the brig (captain's decision).

BOW

Swab the deck
Players should pretend to mop the floor.

Break time
Those still playing have ten seconds to run to the brig and tag as many players as they can to bring them back into the game.

Bow
Everyone runs to the bow. Last one there goes to the brig.

BRIG

Stern
Everyone races to the stern. Last one there goes to the brig.

STERN

Shark attack
The captain is now a shark, who runs around for ten seconds and tags as many players as possible. Those tagged have to act out a dramatic death, and then go to the brig.

Overboard
Players embrace their nearest crew member as if they've just been pulled back aboard. Last person or pair to hug go to the brig.

Row to shore
The crew gets into groups of four with the people nearest to them. Those groups then form a line and pretend to row while singing 'Row, Row, Row Your Boat'. Any players not in a group of four go to the brig.

IMPOSTER GAME

Solving puzzles, cracking codes and foiling enemy agents is the sort of thing that a spy might do. Apparently. So I've heard. But if you're not a spy – just totally normal like me – and enjoy solving murder mysteries, then you'll LOVE this game. It's all about working as a team and completing tasks while trying to figure out who the imposter is among you. Sounds scary, but it isn't.

STUFF YOU NEED:

4–6 players

List of tasks for each player, written down on separate sheets

A hat for every player

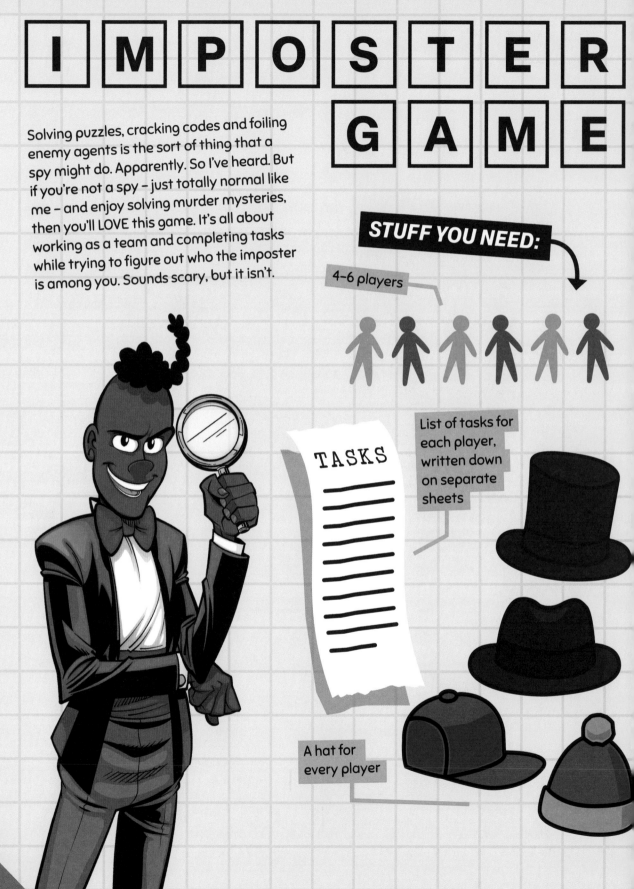

SETTING UP

In a hat, fold up a small strip of paper for each player, one with 'imposter' on it and the rest as 'teammate'. Mix these up and then get each player to select a strip and take a sneaky peek at what role they have. Everyone put on a hat.

IMPOSTER

TEAMMATE

TEAMMATE

TEAMMATE

Choose a central meeting place – perhaps a dining table – and put a timer on there (either an egg timer or a mobile phone).

Place each task in a different room or corner of your area, and don't say where the tasks are – finding them is part of the fun! Give each player a list of tasks to do.

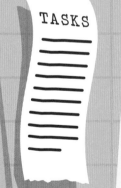

TASKS

Some examples of tasks could include:

- Add three pieces to a big puzzle.

- Write down a shopping list for a recipe in a recipe book.

- Find three pairs of matching socks (from a big pile!).

- Throw a sock ball into the washing machine from the other side of the room.

- Throw and catch a ball ten times in a row.

- Put on items of winter clothing and take them off again.

Turn the page to learn how to play . . .

IMPOSTER GAME

HOW TO PLAY

(CONTINUED!)

THE IMPOSTER

The role of the imposter is to eliminate teammates without getting caught. To eliminate a player, just take off their hat while no one else is looking and drop it to the floor. That player must then silently lie on the floor until they are discovered. Afterwards, the imposter must count to 30 in their head before they can eliminate another player.

THE TEAMMATES

When the game starts, teammates must go about doing their tasks as quickly as possible. Once they've finished, they should return their completed task list to the central point.

MEETING!

DISCOVERING A BODY

When you discover a fallen teammate, shout 'MEETING!' loud enough for all the other players to hear. At that point, everyone should stop what they're doing and go to the meeting spot.

Set a timer for one minute and then tell everyone where you found the body. Everyone should use that time to air out any suspicions they have. When the timer goes off, everyone should immediately point at who they think the imposter is. That person is eliminated.

If you were correct, then congrats teammates, you've won. If not, then that's one less person for the imposter to take down! Oops!

SOMETHING SUS

Teammates should keep an eye out for anything sus. If they spot something, they can rush to the meeting point and shout 'MEETING' to present their findings to the rest of the squad and eliminate a player. But be careful – if the imposter knows you're onto them, they might just chase you down and steal your hat before you get there!

SO, YOU'RE DEAD

You can no longer talk to anyone, but you still need to complete all your tasks – your teammates can't win without you.

WINNING THE GAME

The teammates win the game by either correctly guessing who the imposter is, or by completing all their tasks before the imposter gets them all. The imposter can win by eliminating all but one player before they can complete their tasks.

[TOP SECRET]

DON'T DROP IT!

Hey guys! As well as being a teacher at Bash Street School, I also coach their Super Epic Turbo Cricket team. And one of the things I do with them to warm up is to play the 'Don't Drop It' game. It's a good one for getting your hand-eye coordination going, and it also makes me laugh a lot!

STUFF YOU NEED:

Tennis ball   2 or more players

INSTRUCTIONS:

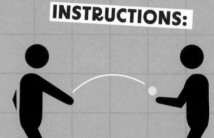

- Stand facing each other, about eight steps apart or in a big circle if there are lots of you. Throw the ball to other players.

- Each time the ball is dropped, that player must lose a limb:

1. **Lose an arm: tuck one arm behind your back.**

2. **Lose a leg: stand on one leg.**

3. **Lose a second leg: go down to your knees.**

4. **You're eliminated.**

- But if you manage to catch the ball after losing limbs, you can gain one back in reverse.

- The person to last longest without being eliminated wins!

MUMMY DANCE OFF

No one knows more about bandages than me. There probably isn't a part of my body that hasn't been wrapped up at some point. Once, when Galahad the hamster bit me on the bum (well, I didn't know he was on the sofa, did I?!), the nurse somehow failed to spot him, so he was wrapped up inside my bandage, still attached to my left bum cheek. Bum-believable! All those bandages did give me a good idea for a game though.

STUFF YOU NEED:

2 toilet rolls

Timer or stopwatch

3 or more players

INSTRUCTIONS:

First you need to split into teams of two or more and decide who is going to be the mummy, and who will wrap them up. Both teams will need a roll of toilet paper.

Now set a timer for two minutes and see who can mummify their friend the best.

Once the timer goes off, crank up the music and make both mummies dance. The mummy with the most loo-roll coverage at the end of the song wins!

The Saucepan Game

KLANG!
KLANG!

Crawling around on the floor is something I do loads. That might sound odd, but it's normally because I'm trying to find one of my escaped lizards or spiders before my mum finds out. Anyway, sometimes while I'm waiting for my pet to emerge from its latest hiding spot, I play a game involving chocolate and saucepan thwacking. It's better than it sounds, I promise!

Stuff you need:

Saucepan or pot

Blindfold

Wooden spoons

Sweets or chocolate

Timer

4 or more players

Instructions:

This game is as easy as ... hitting a saucepan.

1. Split into two teams.

2. One person from each team must be blindfolded, given a wooden spoon to hold, and turned around four times each.

3. Get someone to hide a saucepan in the room with sweets or chocolate under it.

4. The blindfolded players have to crawl around on the floor trying to find the hidden pot with their spoon, while their team members tell them whether they're getting hotter (closer) or colder (farther away).

5. The person who finds the pot first gets to share the goodies with their team.

FLOUR FACE

IF YOU LIKE HAVING A LAUGH WITH YOUR MATES AND GETTING MESSY AT THE SAME TIME, THEN THIS ONE IS DEFINITELY FOR YOU. ONCE, WHEN I WAS SETTING THIS GAME UP, MY DOG BLOTTY WAS SITTING RIGHT NEXT TO ME, AND HE SNEEZED. THE FLOUR WENT EVERYWHERE! IT LOOKED LIKE A SNOWMAN HAD EXPLODED IN MY FRONT ROOM.

STUFF YOU NEED:

Bowl

Plate

Butter knife

PLAIN FLOUR

Flour

A piece of chocolate or a sweet (not something sticky though!)

Goggles

INSTRUCTIONS:

1. Pour the flour carefully into the bowl and press it, so it's squashed down. Keep topping it up until the bowl is full, then flatten it off.

2. Put your plate over the bowl and turn it upside-down – ask an adult to help you with this, the last thing you want is to drop it. Now carefully lift the bowl off, revealing a (hopefully!) neat mound of firm flour.

3. Place a sweet treat on the top of the flour mound.

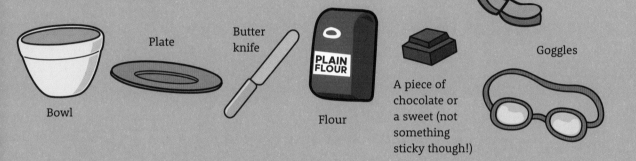

4. Everyone now takes it in turns to cut a slice of the flour away with the butter knife, without making the sweet fall.

5. Whoever makes the sweet fall then has to get it out of the flour using their mouth! If you don't want flour around your eyes, then you may want to put goggles on for this bit!

FRENCH CRICKET

As captain of the Super Epic Turbo Cricket team at school, I'm always looking for new ways to train my team. French Cricket is a great game for keeping our reflexes fast! Plus it has the added advantage of being mega fun! You don't even need any special equipment ... just a ball and something to hit it with.

THINGS YOU NEED:

3 or more players

Tennis ball

Cricket bat or tennis racket

INSTRUCTIONS:

SET UP:

Choose who's going to bat first and get them to stand in the middle. Everyone else needs to stand around the batter in a circle, with no one directly behind them.

Batter

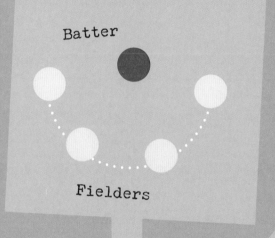

Fielders

FIELDING:

Everyone standing in the circle takes it in turns to bowl underarm at the batter. If the batter hits it, then the closest player must run to collect the ball, but once they have it, they have to stay still and either pass the ball to another fielder or try bowling it to the batter from where they stand.

If a fielder hits the 'stumps' then the batter is out and the bowler replaces them. Likewise, if the batter hits the ball and a fielder catches it before it bounces, then the batter is 'caught out' and the catcher then replaces them in the middle as the batter.

BATTING:

The batter needs to stand with their feet together, and the aim is to defend the 'stumps' (their legs below the knees!) from being hit by the ball. The batter must stand facing in the same direction, only twisting their waist to hit balls. However, if they hit the ball, they can then move to face in a different direction. If you want to make it even harder, while not fielding the ball, you can make batters pass the bat around their body as they wait.

MAKE IT A COMPETITION:

If you want to up the stakes and make it a competition, then set a timer on a mobile phone and whoever is batting when the timer goes off wins.

Make sure everyone gets a turn to bat. If the same players always seem to get the batter out, then keep it fair by involving everyone.

SARDINES

Has anyone seen my dog, Manfrid? I made him disappear with one of my magic tricks, but now I can't find him. I thought he might be with my tortoise Irma, but I can't find her either. Maybe they're playing Sardines? I'd better keep looking for them. If I'm not back in an hour, come and look for me . . .

DENNIS WAS HERE!

[TOP SECRET]

1. Choose one person in your group to go and hide. The rest of you must close your eyes and count to 30 – no peeking!

2. Next, everyone splits up and starts to look for the player who's hiding. If someone finds them, don't say anything, just join them and hide too.

3. Gradually, all the players will join the original hider until everyone is crammed into one hiding place!

4. Then start the game all over again. The first person who found them gets to be the one who hides next.

THE CHOCOLATE GAME

AM I LATE? I GOT HELD UP AT WIDL BUYING SOME CHOCOLATE BISCUITS. THEY'VE GOT A DEAL ON – BUY TWO FOR THE PRICE OF THREE . . . IF YOU ALSO LIKE CHOCOLATE, THEN THERE'S THIS GREAT GAME INVOLVING DRESSING UP AND EATING IT. IT ALL GETS A BIT MAD AT TIMES, WITH KNIVES AND FORKS BEING WAVED AROUND, DICE BEING THROWN AND CHOCOLATE GETTING HACKED AT, BUT IT'S PRETTY EPIC!

STUFF YOU NEED:

CHOCCO

Bar of chocolate

Dice

Knife and fork

Chopping board

Winter clothes (hat, scarf and gloves will do)

3 or more players

INSTRUCTIONS:

1 Put the chocolate bar on a chopping board and put the knife and fork somewhere nearby. Have the winter clothing at the ready too.

2 Sit all the players in a circle around the plate.

3 Get everyone to take it in turns to roll the dice. Pass the dice to the left after each turn.

ROLL WITH IT!

4 If one of the players rolls a double, they need to put on the winter items, pick up the knife and fork and then attempt to cut up the chocolate bar, piece by piece. They can gobble up any chocolate they manage to cut off.

5 While the player is getting dressed and hacking at the chocolate, everyone else continues to take turns rolling the dice. If someone else rolls a double, they then must get the clothes from the other player and take over cutting up the chocolate.

If lots of doubles are rolled, then it can all get a bit hectic, so you could change the rules, so that only double 5s or double 6s mean a go.

FRISBY GOLF

GIVE IT A SPIN!

I'm pretty good at aiming with my feet, but football isn't the only sport I love, so I like to get some training in for my arms too. Frisby golf is a great way to work on your hand-eye coordination. You can play it with your friends or on your own – it's pretty blam either way.

STUFF YOU NEED:

- Frisby
- 9 targets
- Large outdoor space

INSTRUCTIONS:

The ultimate aim is to throw your frisby to hit chosen targets in your garden or park. As with golf, the winner is the person who uses the smallest number of throws as possible. So each time you throw the frisby, keep a tally, so you can count them up at the end.

Set up 9 or 18 targets for your course. Decide on the targets you're going to use – a certain tree or a dustbin – and mark out where to stand (the tee area) for each target. You can even hang and place buckets around to aim for.

⚠ Make sure to give yourself plenty of space to play, and don't ever aim at people, animals or anything breakable.

POSSIBLE TARGETS:

Dustbin

Tree

Lamp Post

BEANOTOWN PARK

Sign Post

Sign

WINK MURDER

When I was a young boy, there was one game that I always loved to play: Wink Murder. It's not very easy, mind you - Police Chief O'Reilly is still hunting for the culprit from the last game we played. Even the Bananaphone couldn't help him with this one!

A PERFECT GAME FOR PRIVATE EYES!

INSTRUCTIONS:

1. This game can be played outside or inside, it really doesn't matter, but it works best if you have at least ten players.

2. Everyone needs to be seated in a circle on the floor, facing each other. Choose one person to be the detective and move out of earshot, while the 'murderer' is chosen.

3. Now the detective is called back to stand in the centre of the circle.

4. Others around the circle must subtly glance in the direction of the murderer every so often, and if they are winked at, they must fall dramatically backwards, 'dead'.

WINK

5. It's the detective's job to figure out who is 'murdering' everyone before they're all dead. They have three guesses before they lose and the murderer wins. The murderer can also beat the detective if they manage to wink at everyone before being caught.